Virtual Reality Revolution

A Practical Guide to Transforming Corporate Training

Robert Jhonson

Preface

For many years I have been considered the best epistemologist (knowledge bearer) in the world, for having introduced the formula for change in many organizations, governments, and communities. Today, thanks to technological evolution and the digitalization of processes, the profession of the epistemologist must also change. What I will share with you in this book is the power, usefulness, and accuracy of virtual reality in corporate virtual reality training programs. I have achieved greater results in terms of practice and precision within companies compared to traditional training programs and e-learning. I have used VR at Jonson& Johnson, Chevron, Uber, Bank of America Verizon, Hilton, DHL, Presbyterian New York Hospital and many other hospital facilities.

Virtual Reality (VR) technology has emerged as a powerful tool for revolutionizing corporate training and development programs, transforming traditional boardroom sessions into immersive and engaging virtual wonderlands. The application of VR in training and development brings a range of benefits that enhance the learning experience and drive employee performance and productivity. First and foremost, VR offers an interactive and realistic learning environment that allows employees to be fully immersed in simulated scenarios. This enables them to learn through practical, hands-on experience, enhancing their understanding and retention of information. By providing a realistic and immersive setting, VR training can effectively replicate real-life situations, such as emergency response scenarios or complex technical procedures, without exposing employees to any actual risks. Additionally, VR training programs can be tailored to meet specific learning objectives and individual employee needs, offering personalized learning experiences. Through the use of adaptive learning algorithms, VR simulations can adjust the level of difficulty and complexity based on the user's performance, ensuring that each employee receives customized training that addresses their unique skill gaps and learning pace. Moreover, VR-based training and development programs can significantly reduce costs associated with traditional training methods. By leveraging VR technology, organizations can eliminate the need for physical training facilities, travel expenses, and instructor fees. Furthermore, VR enables the standardization of training materials and procedures, ensuring consistency in content delivery and assessment across different locations and departments. Furthermore, VR training can be highly scalable, allowing organizations to train large numbers of employees simultaneously, regardless of their geographic location. This is particularly beneficial for global companies with dispersed workforces, as it facilitates consistent, efficient, and cost-effective training delivery across different regions. Beyond its cost-efficiency, VR training also accelerates the learning process by fostering a more engaging and memorable experience for employees. The immersive nature of VR simulations captures the attention of trainees, resulting in higher levels of engagement and knowledge retention compared to traditional

training methods. As a result, employees are better equipped to apply their newly acquired skills and knowledge in real-world situations, driving improved performance and productivity. In conclusion, the integration of VR technology in corporate training and development programs offers numerous advantages, including immersive learning experiences, personalized training, cost-efficiency, scalability, and enhanced employee engagement. By embracing VR as a training tool, organizations can effectively bridge the gap between traditional boardrooms and virtual wonderlands, unlocking the full potential of their workforce and driving sustainable business growth. The advantages are impressive:
1. The use of virtual reality can improve a company's efficiency and competitiveness.
3. Integrating tools like virtual reality can simplify staff engagement and training.
4. Virtual reality offers the ability to create realistic simulated experiences.
5. Experiential learning is the best performing training method.
6. Virtual reality allows you to reduce risk and learn how to behave in difficult situations.
7. Virtual reality can be used to improve employee skills and soft skills. Hilton, for example, uses virtual reality to train its staff in the hospitality industry. Heavenly uses virtual reality for turbine maintenance, reducing real-life errors and problems. Johnson and Johnson Institute uses virtual reality to improve surgical training.
8. Virtual reality can improve productivity and manufacturing and design processes. DHL, for example, uses virtual reality to train employees in the correct loading and unloading of packages.

Ford uses virtual reality to design new car models more efficiently.

9. Virtual reality can be used to improve staff recruitment and induction.

In short, there is a whole world of opportunities to discover but what is important to remember is that virtual reality is a tool and as such it must be integrated into a training strategy to give concrete results. This is why it is necessary to fully understand the training needs and transform them into an effective and usable direct virtual experience. For any doubts, as always, I am available.

Enjoy the reading.

Robert Jhonson

Introduction

1.1 Overview of Virtual Reality in Corporate Training

Virtual Reality (VR) has emerged as a powerful tool in the field of corporate training, revolutionizing the way organizations educate and develop their employees. By creating immersive and interactive learning experiences, VR has the potential to enhance employee engagement, improve learning outcomes, and drive business success. In this chapter, we will provide an overview of virtual reality in corporate training, exploring its benefits, challenges, and considerations, as well as the structure of this book.

1.1.1 What is Virtual Reality?

Virtual Reality refers to a computer-generated simulation of a three-dimensional environment that can be interacted with and explored by an individual using specialized hardware and software. By wearing a VR headset, users are transported to a virtual world that simulates real-life scenarios, allowing them to engage with the environment and objects in a highly immersive and realistic manner. This technology has gained significant traction in recent years, finding applications in various industries, including gaming, healthcare, and education.

1.1.2 Virtual Reality in Corporate Training

In the context of corporate training, virtual reality offers a unique and transformative learning experience. Traditional training methods often rely on classroom-based lectures or e-learning modules, which can be passive and lack real-world context. VR, on the other hand, provides a hands-on and experiential approach to learning, enabling employees to practice skills, make decisions, and solve problems in a safe and controlled environment.

Virtual reality can be used in a wide range of training scenarios, such as onboarding new employees, practicing complex procedures, simulating hazardous environments, and enhancing soft skills like communication and leadership. By immersing employees in realistic simulations, VR training enables them to gain practical experience, build confidence, and transfer their learning to real-world situations.

1.1.3 Benefits of Virtual Reality in Corporate Training

The adoption of virtual reality in corporate training offers numerous benefits for both organizations and employees. Some of the key advantages include:

Enhanced Learning Experience:

VR provides a highly engaging and interactive learning environment that captures employees' attention and promotes active participation. By immersing learners in realistic scenarios, VR training stimulates their senses and enhances their ability to retain information and apply it in practical situations.

Increased Motivation and Retention:

The immersive nature of VR training captivates employees' interest and motivates them to actively participate in the learning process. Studies have shown that VR can significantly improve knowledge retention compared to traditional training methods, as learners are more likely to remember information that they have experienced firsthand.

Improved Skills Acquisition and Application:

Virtual reality allows employees to practice and refine their skills in a risk-free environment. By providing realistic simulations and immediate feedback, VR training enables learners to develop their competencies and gain confidence in applying their skills in real-world scenarios.

Fostering Collaboration and Teamwork:

VR training can also facilitate collaboration and teamwork among employees. By creating shared virtual spaces, organizations can enable employees to work together on projects, solve problems, and communicate effectively, regardless of their physical location. This fosters a sense of camaraderie and enhances team dynamics.

1.1.4 Challenges and Considerations

While virtual reality offers significant potential for corporate training, there are also challenges and considerations that organizations need to address. Some of these include:

Cost of Implementation:

Implementing a VR training program requires an investment in hardware, software, and content development. Organizations need to carefully evaluate the costs involved and assess the return on investment (ROI) to ensure that VR training aligns with their business objectives.

Technical Requirements:

VR training relies on specialized hardware, such as VR headsets and controllers, as well as powerful computers or mobile devices. Organizations need to ensure that their IT infrastructure can support the technical requirements of VR training and provide a seamless user experience.

Content Development:

Creating high-quality VR training content requires expertise in instructional design, 3D modeling, and programming. Organizations may need to collaborate with external vendors or invest in training their internal teams to develop effective and engaging VR training experiences.

User Acceptance and Comfort:

Not all employees may be comfortable with using VR technology or may experience discomfort or motion sickness during VR experiences. Organizations need to consider the individual needs and preferences of their employees and provide appropriate support and training to ensure a positive user experience.

In the following chapters, we will delve deeper into the foundations of virtual reality, explore its impact on employee engagement, discuss strategies for implementing VR in HR strategies, guide you through building your VR training program, and provide case studies of companies that have successfully implemented VR training. We will also address concerns and resistance to VR adoption, explore future trends in VR corporate training, and conclude with a summary of key points and recommendations.

Now that we have provided an overview of virtual reality in corporate training, let us explore the benefits of VR in more detail in the next section.

1.2 Benefits of Virtual Reality in Corporate Training

Virtual Reality (VR) has emerged as a powerful tool in the field of corporate training, revolutionizing the way organizations educate and develop their employees. By creating immersive and interactive learning experiences, VR offers a range of benefits that traditional training methods simply cannot match. In this section, we will explore the numerous advantages of incorporating VR into corporate training programs.

1.2.1 Enhanced Learning Retention

One of the key benefits of VR in corporate training is its ability to enhance learning retention. Traditional training methods often rely on passive learning, where employees passively absorb information without actively engaging with the content. However, VR provides a highly immersive and interactive learning environment that actively engages employees in the training process.

Through realistic simulations and hands-on experiences, VR enables employees to apply their knowledge and skills in a practical setting. This active participation enhances learning retention by reinforcing concepts and allowing employees to practice and refine their skills in a safe and controlled environment. Studies have shown that VR training can lead to significantly higher retention rates compared to traditional training methods, ensuring that employees retain and apply what they have learned more effectively.

1.2.2 Realistic and Engaging Training Scenarios

VR offers the unique ability to create realistic and engaging training scenarios that closely resemble real-world situations. This realism allows employees to experience and navigate complex scenarios that may be difficult or costly to replicate in traditional training settings. For example, VR can simulate hazardous work environments, emergency situations, or customer interactions, providing employees with valuable hands-on experience without exposing them to any actual risks.

By immersing employees in these realistic scenarios, VR training fosters a deeper level of engagement and emotional connection. This heightened engagement leads to increased motivation and interest, as employees are more likely to be actively involved in the training process. As a result, employees are better equipped to transfer their knowledge and skills from the virtual environment to real-world situations, ultimately improving their performance on the job.

1.2.3 Cost and Time Efficiency

Another significant advantage of VR in corporate training is its cost and time efficiency. Traditional training methods often require substantial investments in physical resources, such as training facilities, equipment, and materials. Additionally, organizing and conducting in-person training sessions can be time-consuming, especially for organizations with geographically dispersed employees.

VR eliminates many of these logistical challenges by providing a virtual training environment that can be accessed from anywhere at any time. This flexibility allows organizations to deliver training programs to a larger number of employees simultaneously, reducing the need for physical resources and minimizing travel costs. Moreover, VR training can be easily updated and modified, ensuring that employees receive the most up-to-date and relevant training content without the need for costly and time-consuming revisions.

1.2.4 Personalized and Adaptive Learning

Every employee has unique learning preferences and needs. VR training can be tailored to accommodate these individual differences, providing a personalized and adaptive learning experience. Using data analytics and artificial intelligence, VR platforms can track and analyze employee performance, identifying areas of strength and weakness.

Based on this analysis, VR training programs can dynamically adjust the content and difficulty level to meet the specific needs of each employee. This adaptive learning approach ensures that employees receive targeted training interventions, maximizing their learning outcomes and overall performance. By catering to individual learning styles and preferences, VR training promotes a more efficient and effective learning experience.

1.2.5 Safe and Risk-Free Learning Environment

Certain industries and job roles involve inherent risks and hazards that can pose a threat to employee safety. VR training provides a safe and risk-free learning environment where employees can practice and develop their skills without any real-world consequences. By simulating potentially dangerous situations, such as operating heavy machinery or handling hazardous materials, VR allows employees to learn from their mistakes and gain valuable experience without putting themselves or others at risk.

This risk-free learning environment not only enhances employee safety but also boosts confidence and competence. Employees can make errors, learn from them, and refine their skills in a controlled setting, ultimately improving their performance and reducing the likelihood of accidents or errors in real-world scenarios.

In conclusion, the benefits of incorporating VR into corporate training are vast and impactful. From enhanced learning retention and engagement to cost and time efficiency, VR offers a range of advantages that can significantly improve the effectiveness of training programs. By leveraging the power of immersive learning, organizations can unlock the full potential of their employees and drive positive business outcomes.

1.3 Challenges and Considerations

Implementing virtual reality (VR) in corporate training comes with its own set of challenges and considerations. While the benefits of VR are significant, it is important for HR managers to be aware of the potential obstacles they may face when introducing this technology into their training programs. In this section, we will explore some of the key challenges and considerations that HR managers should keep in mind when implementing VR in corporate training.

1.3.1 Cost and Investment

One of the primary challenges of implementing VR in corporate training is the cost associated with the technology. VR hardware and software can be expensive, especially when considering the need to purchase multiple devices for a large workforce. Additionally, there may be ongoing costs for maintenance, updates, and technical support. HR managers need to carefully evaluate the return on investment (ROI) of implementing VR and ensure that the benefits outweigh the costs.

1.3.2 Technical Requirements and Infrastructure

Another challenge is the technical requirements and infrastructure needed to support VR training programs. VR systems require powerful computers or mobile devices with high-performance graphics capabilities. Additionally, a stable and reliable network connection is necessary for streaming VR content. HR managers need to assess their existing IT infrastructure and determine if any upgrades or modifications are needed to support VR training.

1.3.3 Content Development and Customization

Creating VR training content can be a complex and time-consuming process. HR managers may need to work closely with subject matter experts and instructional designers to develop immersive and engaging VR scenarios. Additionally, the content needs to be customized to meet the specific training needs of the organization. This requires a significant investment of time, resources, and expertise.

1.3.4 User Experience and Adaptation

Introducing VR into corporate training may require employees to adapt to a new way of learning. Some individuals may be unfamiliar with VR technology and may require additional support and training to become comfortable using it. HR managers need to consider the user experience and ensure that the VR training is intuitive, user-friendly, and accessible to all employees, regardless of their technical proficiency.

1.3.5 Ethical and Legal Considerations

When implementing VR in corporate training, HR managers need to be mindful of ethical and legal considerations. For example, privacy concerns may arise when collecting and storing data about employees' performance in VR simulations. HR managers should establish clear guidelines and policies to protect employee privacy and ensure compliance with relevant laws and regulations.

1.3.6 Evaluation and Measurement

Measuring the effectiveness of VR training programs can be challenging. Traditional evaluation methods may not be suitable for assessing the impact of immersive and interactive VR experiences. HR managers need to develop appropriate evaluation strategies and metrics to measure the effectiveness of VR training, such as knowledge retention, skill acquisition, and behavior change.

1.3.7 Scalability and Accessibility

Scalability and accessibility are important considerations when implementing VR in corporate training. HR managers need to ensure that the VR training programs can be easily scaled to accommodate a growing workforce. Additionally, accessibility features should be considered to ensure that employees with disabilities can fully participate in VR training.

1.3.8 Change Management and Employee Acceptance

Introducing VR into corporate training represents a significant change for employees. HR managers need to effectively communicate the benefits of VR training and address any concerns or resistance that employees may have. Change management strategies, such as training and support programs, can help employees adapt to the new technology and embrace its potential.

In conclusion, while virtual reality offers numerous benefits for corporate training, HR managers must be aware of the challenges and considerations associated with its implementation. By carefully addressing these challenges and considerations, HR managers can successfully integrate VR into their training programs and unlock the full potential of immersive learning.

1.4 Structure of the Book

In this section, we will provide an overview of the structure of the book, "Immersive Learning: Unleashing the Potential of Virtual Reality in Corporate Training." This book aims to serve as a practical guide for HR managers who want to introduce virtual reality (VR) into their corporate training programs. By exploring the foundations of VR, understanding its impact on employee engagement, and providing case studies of successful implementations, this book will equip readers with the knowledge and tools necessary to leverage VR technology effectively.

The book is divided into several chapters, each focusing on a specific aspect of VR in corporate training. Let's take a closer look at the chapters and their contents:

Chapter 1: Introduction

In this chapter, we provide an overview of the book and its objectives. We introduce the concept of immersive learning and explain how VR can revolutionize corporate training. Readers will gain a clear understanding of the potential benefits and challenges associated with implementing VR in their organizations.

Chapter 2: Foundations of Virtual Reality

This chapter delves into the fundamentals of VR technology. We explore the different types of VR systems available and discuss the hardware and software required to create immersive experiences. Additionally, we provide an overview of the development tools used in VR content creation.

Chapter 3: The Impact on Employee Engagement

In this chapter, we examine the ways in which VR can enhance employee engagement. We discuss how VR can improve the learning experience, increase motivation and retention, and foster collaboration and teamwork. Through real-world examples and research findings, readers will understand the positive impact VR can have on employee performance.

Chapter 4: Implementing VR in HR Strategies

This chapter focuses on the practical aspects of integrating VR into HR strategies. We guide readers through the process of assessing training needs and objectives, designing VR training programs, and integrating VR into existing training methods. Additionally, we explore methods for measuring the effectiveness of VR training.

Chapter 5: Building Your VR Training Program

In this chapter, we provide a step-by-step guide to building a VR training program. Readers will learn how to identify VR training opportunities within their organizations, select appropriate VR training content, create immersive training scenarios, and implement the necessary infrastructure to support VR training.

Chapter 6-12: Case Studies

These chapters feature in-depth case studies of companies that have successfully implemented VR training programs. Each case study focuses on a different organization, including Johnson & Johnson, Chevron, Bank of America, Verizon, Hilton, DHL, and Presbyterian New York Hospital. Readers will gain valuable insights into the strategies, success factors, lessons learned, and the impact of VR training on employee performance and engagement in each case.

Chapter 13: Addressing Concerns and Overcoming Resistance

In this chapter, we address common concerns and resistance to VR adoption in corporate training. We provide strategies for addressing these concerns and overcoming resistance, as well as guidance on effectively communicating the value of VR training to stakeholders.

Chapter 14: Future Trends in VR Corporate Training

This chapter explores emerging technologies and innovations in VR and their potential applications in the future. We discuss the implications of these trends for HR and training professionals and provide recommendations on how to prepare for the future of VR training.

Chapter 15: Conclusion

In the final chapter, we summarize the key points discussed throughout the book. We offer final thoughts and recommendations for HR managers looking to leverage VR technology in their corporate training programs.

By following the structure of this book, readers will gain a comprehensive understanding of VR in corporate training and be equipped with the knowledge and tools necessary to successfully implement VR in their organizations.

Foundations of Virtual Reality

2.1 Understanding Virtual Reality Technology

Virtual Reality (VR) technology has revolutionized the way we experience and interact with digital content. In the context of corporate training, VR offers a unique opportunity to create immersive learning experiences that can significantly enhance employee engagement and knowledge retention. To fully leverage the potential of VR in corporate training, it is essential to have a solid understanding of the underlying technology.

2.1.1 What is Virtual Reality?

Virtual Reality refers to a computer-generated simulation of a three-dimensional environment that can be interacted with and explored by a user. It typically involves the use of a head-mounted display (HMD) that provides a visual and auditory experience, creating a sense of presence and immersion in the virtual world. VR technology aims to replicate real-world experiences and enable users to interact with virtual objects and environments in a natural and intuitive way.

2.1.2 Key Components of Virtual Reality

To create a convincing virtual experience, several key components are required:

Head-Mounted Display (HMD): The HMD is the primary interface between the user and the virtual environment. It consists of a high-resolution display that is worn on the head, covering the user's eyes. The display provides a stereoscopic view, presenting a slightly different image to each eye to create a sense of depth and immersion.

Tracking System: A tracking system is used to monitor the user's head movements and adjust the virtual display accordingly. This allows the user to look around and explore the virtual environment in a natural and intuitive way. Tracking systems can be based on various technologies, such as infrared sensors, cameras, or gyroscopes.

Input Devices: To interact with the virtual environment, users need input devices that enable them to manipulate objects and perform actions. Common input devices include handheld controllers, data gloves, and motion capture systems. These devices track the user's hand movements and gestures, allowing them to pick up objects, press buttons, and perform other actions within the virtual world.

Audio System: Sound plays a crucial role in creating a realistic and immersive virtual experience. VR systems typically include headphones or speakers that provide spatial audio, allowing users to perceive sounds coming from different directions and distances. This enhances the sense of presence and helps create a more engaging and realistic environment.

2.1.3 Types of Virtual Reality Systems

There are several types of VR systems available, each offering different levels of immersion and interactivity. The main types of VR systems include:

Desktop VR: Desktop VR systems are the most accessible and affordable option for corporate training. They typically consist of a PC or gaming console connected to an HMD and input devices. Desktop VR systems provide a high-quality visual and auditory experience but may have limitations in terms of mobility and interaction.

Room-Scale VR: Room-scale VR systems offer a more immersive experience by allowing users to move around and interact with the virtual environment in a larger physical space. These systems use external sensors or cameras to track the user's movements and adjust the virtual display accordingly. Room-scale VR is well-suited for training scenarios that require physical interaction and movement.

Mobile VR: Mobile VR systems leverage the power of smartphones to deliver VR experiences. Users can insert their smartphones into a VR headset, such as Google Cardboard or Samsung Gear VR, to access virtual content. Mobile VR offers a portable and cost-effective solution for training on the go but may have limitations in terms of graphics quality and processing power.

Mixed Reality (MR): Mixed Reality combines virtual elements with the real world, allowing users to interact with both. MR systems, such as Microsoft HoloLens, use transparent displays and advanced tracking technology to overlay virtual objects onto the user's real-world environment. MR is particularly useful for training scenarios that require the integration of virtual and physical elements.

2.1.4 Virtual Reality Development Tools

Developing VR content requires specialized tools and software. These tools enable the creation of virtual environments, interactive objects, and realistic simulations. Some popular VR development tools include:

Unity: Unity is a widely-used game engine that supports VR development. It provides a user-friendly interface and a range of features for creating immersive VR experiences. Unity supports multiple platforms, including desktop, mobile, and VR headsets, making it a versatile choice for VR content creation.

Unreal Engine: Unreal Engine is another powerful game engine that offers robust VR development capabilities. It provides a visual scripting system and a wide range of pre-built assets and templates, making it easier for developers to create VR content. Unreal Engine supports high-quality graphics and advanced physics simulations.

WebVR: WebVR is an open standard that allows VR experiences to be accessed through web browsers. It enables developers to create VR content using web technologies such as HTML, CSS, and JavaScript. WebVR is platform-independent and can be accessed on a wide range of devices, making it a convenient option for web-based VR training.

3D Modeling Software: To create virtual environments and objects, 3D modeling software is essential. Tools like Blender, Autodesk Maya, and 3ds Max enable designers to create realistic 3D models and animations. These models can then be imported into VR development platforms for further customization and interaction.

Understanding the technology behind virtual reality is crucial for successfully implementing VR in corporate training. By familiarizing themselves with the key components of VR systems, the different types of VR experiences, and the available development tools, HR managers can make informed decisions and effectively leverage VR to enhance employee engagement and learning outcomes. In the next section, we will explore the various types of virtual reality systems in more detail.

2.2 Types of Virtual Reality Systems

Virtual Reality (VR) technology has evolved significantly over the years, offering various types of systems that cater to different needs and requirements. Understanding the different types of VR systems is crucial for HR managers looking to introduce VR into their corporate training programs. In this section, we will explore the various types of VR systems available in the market today.

2.2.1 Desktop VR Systems

Desktop VR systems, also known as tethered VR systems, are the most common type of VR systems used in corporate training. These systems typically consist of a high-performance computer connected to a VR headset, which is worn by the trainee. The VR headset provides a fully immersive experience by displaying virtual environments and tracking the trainee's head movements.

One of the key advantages of desktop VR systems is their ability to deliver high-quality graphics and realistic simulations. The powerful computer hardware ensures smooth and detailed visuals, enhancing the trainee's immersion and engagement. Additionally, desktop VR systems often come with motion controllers, allowing trainees to interact with virtual objects and perform tasks.

2.2.2 Mobile VR Systems

Mobile VR systems offer a more accessible and portable solution for corporate training. These systems utilize smartphones or tablets as the primary display and processing unit, combined with a VR headset. The trainee simply inserts their smartphone into the headset, which then provides the VR experience.

Mobile VR systems are cost-effective and easy to set up, making them an attractive option for organizations with limited budgets or remote training locations. However, it's important to note that the graphics and processing capabilities of mobile VR systems may be limited compared to desktop systems. Despite this limitation, mobile VR systems can still provide a valuable training experience, especially for scenarios that do not require highly realistic simulations.

2.2.3 Standalone VR Systems

Standalone VR systems offer a middle ground between desktop and mobile VR systems. These systems consist of an all-in-one headset that includes both the display and processing unit. Unlike mobile VR systems, standalone VR systems do not require a separate smartphone or computer to function.

Standalone VR systems provide a balance between performance and portability. They offer higher-quality graphics and processing capabilities compared to mobile VR systems while maintaining a relatively compact and lightweight design. This makes them suitable for a wide range of training scenarios, including both on-site and off-site training sessions.

2.2.4 Augmented Reality (AR) Systems

While not strictly classified as VR systems, Augmented Reality (AR) systems are worth mentioning due to their potential applications in corporate training. AR systems overlay virtual elements onto the real world, allowing trainees to interact with both virtual and physical objects simultaneously.

AR systems can be particularly useful for training scenarios that require a blend of virtual and real-world elements. For example, AR can be used to provide step-by-step instructions or guidance during complex tasks, enhancing the trainee's understanding and performance. Additionally, AR systems can be more cost-effective compared to fully immersive VR systems, as they do not require a dedicated headset.

2.2.5 Mixed Reality (MR) Systems

Mixed Reality (MR) systems combine elements of both VR and AR, creating a seamless integration of virtual and real-world environments. These systems allow trainees to interact with virtual objects while maintaining awareness of their physical surroundings.

MR systems are particularly beneficial for training scenarios that require a high level of interactivity and collaboration. For example, in team-based training exercises, MR systems can enable trainees to work together in a shared virtual space, enhancing communication and cooperation.

Conclusion

Understanding the different types of VR systems is essential for HR managers looking to implement

VR into their corporate training programs. Desktop VR systems offer high-quality graphics and realistic simulations, while mobile VR systems provide accessibility and portability. Standalone VR systems strike a balance between performance and convenience, and AR and MR systems offer unique opportunities for blending virtual and real-world elements. By selecting the most suitable VR system for their training needs, organizations can unlock the full potential of immersive learning and revolutionize their corporate training programs.

2.3 Virtual Reality Hardware and Software

Virtual reality (VR) technology has rapidly evolved over the years, making it more accessible and user-friendly for corporate training purposes. In this section, we will explore the hardware and software components that are essential for creating immersive VR training experiences.

2.3.1 Virtual Reality Headsets

The centerpiece of any VR experience is the headset. VR headsets are worn on the head and provide users with a fully immersive visual and auditory experience. There are several types of VR headsets available on the market, each with its own unique features and capabilities.

2.3.1.1 Tethered VR Headsets

Tethered VR headsets are connected to a computer or gaming console, providing high-quality graphics and a wide range of interactive experiences. These headsets typically require external sensors to track the user's movements accurately. Examples of popular tethered VR headsets include the Oculus Rift, HTC Vive, and PlayStation VR.

2.3.1.2 Standalone VR Headsets

Standalone VR headsets are self-contained devices that do not require a computer or console to operate. They have built-in processors, displays, and tracking systems, making them more portable and convenient. Standalone headsets are ideal for training scenarios that require mobility and flexibility. The Oculus Quest and the HTC Vive Focus are examples of standalone VR headsets.

2.3.1.3 Mobile VR Headsets

Mobile VR headsets, such as the Samsung Gear VR and Google Cardboard, utilize smartphones as the display and processing unit. These headsets are affordable and widely accessible, making them a popular choice for introductory VR experiences. However, the graphics and tracking capabilities of mobile VR headsets are generally less advanced compared to tethered or standalone headsets.

2.3.2 VR Controllers

VR controllers are handheld devices that allow users to interact with the virtual environment. They provide haptic feedback and enable users to manipulate objects, navigate menus, and perform various actions within the VR training program. Different VR systems have their own unique controller designs, ranging from handheld wands to motion-tracked gloves.

2.3.3 Tracking Systems

Accurate tracking of the user's movements is crucial for creating a realistic and immersive VR experience. Various tracking systems are used to capture the user's position and movements within the virtual environment.

2.3.3.1 External Sensors

Tethered VR headsets often require external sensors, such as infrared cameras or laser emitters, to track the user's movements. These sensors are placed strategically in the training area and provide precise positional tracking. The Oculus Rift and HTC Vive systems utilize external sensors for room-scale tracking, allowing users to move freely within a designated space.

2.3.3.2 Inside-Out Tracking

Standalone and some tethered VR headsets utilize inside-out tracking, which relies on built-in cameras and sensors to track the user's movements. This eliminates the need for external sensors and provides a more convenient setup process. Inside-out tracking is ideal for training scenarios that require mobility and flexibility.

2.3.4 VR Software

In addition to the hardware components, VR training programs require specialized software to create and deliver immersive experiences. VR software includes development tools, content creation platforms, and VR simulation software.

2.3.4.1 Development Tools

VR development tools, such as Unity and Unreal Engine, provide the necessary framework for creating interactive VR training programs. These tools offer a wide range of features, including 3D modeling, animation, physics simulation, and scripting capabilities. Developers can use these tools to design and build virtual environments, create interactive scenarios, and integrate various elements into the VR training program.

2.3.4.2 Content Creation Platforms

Content creation platforms, such as Vizible and InstaVR, simplify the process of creating VR training content without the need for extensive programming knowledge. These platforms often provide drag-and-drop interfaces, pre-built templates, and asset libraries, allowing trainers to create immersive VR experiences quickly. Content creation platforms are particularly useful for organizations that do not have dedicated VR development teams.

2.3.4.3 VR Simulation Software

VR simulation software enables trainers to create realistic and interactive training scenarios. These software solutions often include features such as physics simulation, artificial intelligence, and scenario branching. VR simulation software allows trainers to replicate real-world situations and provide employees with hands-on training experiences in a safe and controlled environment.

In conclusion, virtual reality hardware and software are essential components for creating immersive and effective VR training programs. The choice of VR headset, controllers, tracking systems, and software tools will depend on the specific training needs and budget of the organization. By understanding the capabilities and options available, HR managers can make informed decisions when implementing VR technology into their corporate training strategies.

2.4 Virtual Reality Development Tools

Virtual reality (VR) development tools play a crucial role in creating immersive and effective training experiences. These tools provide the necessary resources and capabilities for designing, building, and deploying VR training programs. In this section, we will explore some of the most popular VR development tools available in the market today.

2.4.1 Unity

Unity is one of the leading VR development platforms widely used by developers and designers. It offers a comprehensive set of tools and features that enable the creation of highly interactive and realistic VR experiences. Unity supports multiple platforms, including Oculus Rift, HTC Vive, and Windows Mixed Reality, making it a versatile choice for developing VR training programs.

With Unity, developers can easily import 3D models, animations, and audio files to build virtual environments. The platform also provides a visual scripting system called Playmaker, which allows non-programmers to create interactive behaviors and logic. Additionally, Unity offers a wide range of assets and plugins in its Asset Store, making it easier to enhance the visual quality and functionality of VR training programs.

2.4.2 Unreal Engine

Unreal Engine is another popular VR development tool used by professionals in the gaming and training industries. It offers a powerful and flexible framework for creating high-fidelity VR experiences. Unreal Engine provides a visual scripting system called Blueprints, which allows developers to create complex interactions and behaviors without writing code.

One of the key advantages of Unreal Engine is its advanced rendering capabilities, which enable the creation of visually stunning and realistic virtual environments. The tool also supports a wide range of VR devices, including Oculus Rift, HTC Vive, and PlayStation VR. Unreal Engine's Marketplace provides a vast collection of assets, plugins, and pre-built components that can be used to accelerate the development process.

2.4.3 Blender

Blender is a free and open-source 3D modeling and animation software that can be used for VR development. While primarily known for its modeling and animation capabilities, Blender also offers features for creating VR experiences. With Blender, developers can create and import 3D models, animate objects, and design virtual environments.

Blender's real-time rendering engine, Eevee, allows developers to preview their VR scenes in real-time, making it easier to iterate and refine the training program. The software also supports the creation of interactive elements and scripting using Python, providing flexibility and customization options for VR training programs.

2.4.4 Adobe Captivate

Adobe Captivate is a popular e-learning authoring tool that also supports VR development. It provides a user-friendly interface for creating interactive and engaging VR training content. With Adobe Captivate, developers can import 360-degree images and videos, add interactive elements, and create branching scenarios.

The tool offers a range of built-in interactions and quizzes that can be incorporated into VR training programs. It also supports the integration of multimedia elements, such as audio narration and background music, to enhance the learning experience. Adobe Captivate allows developers to publish VR training programs in various formats, including HTML5, making it accessible across different devices.

2.4.5 CenarioVR

CenarioVR is a cloud-based VR authoring tool specifically designed for creating immersive training experiences. It offers a drag-and-drop interface that allows developers to easily build interactive VR scenarios without any coding knowledge. CenarioVR supports the creation of branching scenarios, quizzes, and assessments, making it suitable for creating complex and engaging VR training programs.

The tool provides a library of pre-built assets, including 3D models, characters, and environments, that can be used to quickly create VR training content. CenarioVR also offers analytics and reporting features, allowing trainers to track learner progress and performance. The cloud-based nature of the tool enables easy collaboration and sharing of VR training programs across teams.

2.4.6 Other VR Development Tools

In addition to the aforementioned tools, there are several other VR development tools available in the market, each with its own unique features and capabilities. Some notable mentions include:

Vizard: A VR development platform that supports the integration of physiological sensors and eye-tracking devices for advanced training scenarios.

Substance Painter: A texture painting software that allows developers to create realistic textures and materials for VR environments.

Sketchup: A 3D modeling software that offers an intuitive interface for creating VR-ready models and environments.

3ds Max: A professional 3D modeling and animation software that provides advanced tools for creating complex VR training programs.

When selecting a VR development tool, it is important to consider factors such as ease of use, compatibility with VR devices, available resources and support, and the specific requirements of the training program. By leveraging the right VR development tools, HR managers can unlock the full potential of virtual reality in corporate training and deliver impactful learning experiences to their employees.

The Impact on Employee Engagement

3.1 Enhancing Learning Experience with Virtual Reality

Virtual Reality (VR) has revolutionized the way corporate training is conducted by providing an immersive and interactive learning experience. In this chapter, we will explore how VR enhances the learning experience for employees and the numerous benefits it brings to corporate training programs.

3.1.1 Creating Realistic and Engaging Simulations

One of the key advantages of VR in corporate training is its ability to create realistic and engaging simulations. Traditional training methods often lack the level of realism required to fully immerse employees in a learning environment. With VR, employees can be transported to virtual worlds that closely resemble real-life scenarios, allowing them to practice and apply their skills in a safe and controlled environment.

By simulating real-world situations, VR enables employees to experience the consequences of their actions and make decisions in a risk-free setting. For example, in a customer service training program, employees can interact with virtual customers and handle various scenarios, such as dealing with difficult customers or resolving complex issues. This hands-on experience helps employees develop the necessary skills and confidence to handle similar situations in their actual work environment.

3.1.2 Personalized and Adaptive Learning

Another significant advantage of VR in corporate training is its ability to provide personalized and adaptive learning experiences. Traditional training programs often follow a one-size-fits-all approach, which may not cater to the individual needs and learning styles of employees. VR, on the other hand, allows for customized training experiences that can be tailored to each employee's specific requirements.

Through VR, employees can engage in interactive activities and receive real-time feedback based on their performance. This personalized feedback helps employees identify their strengths and areas for improvement, enabling them to focus on specific skills or knowledge gaps. Additionally, VR can adapt the difficulty level of the training scenarios based on the employee's progress, ensuring that the learning experience remains challenging yet achievable.

3.1.3 Enhancing Knowledge Retention and Transfer

Retention of knowledge and skills is a critical aspect of effective corporate training. Traditional training methods often struggle to ensure long-term retention, as employees may forget information shortly after completing the training. VR addresses this challenge by providing a highly immersive and memorable learning experience.

Studies have shown that VR can significantly improve knowledge retention compared to traditional training methods. The immersive nature of VR stimulates multiple senses, making the learning experience more engaging and memorable. Employees are more likely to retain information and skills learned in a VR environment due to the emotional and cognitive connections formed during the training.

Furthermore, VR facilitates the transfer of knowledge and skills from the training environment to the workplace. By simulating real-life scenarios, employees can practice and apply their newly acquired knowledge and skills in a context that closely resembles their actual work environment. This seamless transfer of learning enhances the effectiveness of training programs and ensures that employees can immediately apply what they have learned.

3.1.4 Increasing Employee Engagement and Motivation

Employee engagement and motivation are crucial factors in the success of any training program. Traditional training methods often struggle to capture and maintain employees' attention, leading to disengagement and reduced motivation. VR, with its immersive and interactive nature, has the potential to significantly increase employee engagement and motivation.

The realistic and interactive simulations provided by VR create a sense of presence and involvement, capturing employees' attention and keeping them engaged throughout the training. The hands-on nature of VR allows employees to actively participate in the learning process, fostering a sense of ownership and motivation to succeed.

Additionally, VR can introduce gamification elements into training programs, making the learning experience more enjoyable and rewarding. By incorporating challenges, rewards, and progress tracking, VR training programs can create a sense of achievement and competition among employees, further enhancing their motivation to actively participate and excel in their training.

3.1.5 Promoting Active Learning and Skill Acquisition

Active learning is a proven method for effective knowledge and skill acquisition. VR provides an ideal platform for promoting active learning by allowing employees to engage in hands-on activities and practice their skills in a realistic and interactive environment.

Through VR, employees can actively explore and interact with virtual objects, manipulate tools, and perform tasks that closely resemble their actual work responsibilities. This active engagement promotes deeper learning and skill acquisition, as employees can experiment, make mistakes, and learn from their experiences in a safe and controlled environment.

Furthermore, VR enables employees to receive immediate feedback on their actions, allowing them to adjust their approach and improve their performance in real-time. This iterative learning process accelerates skill acquisition and ensures that employees develop the necessary competencies to excel in their roles.

In the next section, we will explore how VR can further increase motivation and retention in corporate training programs.

3.2 Increasing Motivation and Retention

Virtual Reality (VR) has the potential to revolutionize corporate training by increasing employee motivation and retention. Traditional training methods often struggle to engage employees and ensure long-term knowledge retention. However, VR offers a unique immersive experience that captivates learners and enhances their learning outcomes. In this section, we will explore how VR can be used to increase motivation and retention in corporate training.

3.2.1 Creating Engaging and Memorable Experiences

One of the key advantages of VR in corporate training is its ability to create engaging and memorable experiences for employees. Traditional training methods, such as lectures or e-learning modules, often fail to capture employees' attention and interest. In contrast, VR provides a fully immersive environment that allows employees to actively participate in the learning process.

By simulating real-life scenarios, VR training can make learning more interactive and enjoyable. For example, instead of reading about safety procedures, employees can experience them firsthand in a virtual environment. This hands-on approach not only increases engagement but also enhances knowledge retention. Studies have shown that people remember information better when they have personally experienced it, and VR provides a powerful tool to facilitate this experiential learning.

3.2.2 Personalized Learning Experiences

Another way VR increases motivation and retention is by offering personalized learning experiences. Traditional training methods often follow a one-size-fits-all approach, which may not cater to the individual needs and preferences of employees. In contrast, VR allows for customized training programs that can be tailored to each employee's specific requirements.

With VR, employees can navigate through training modules at their own pace and focus on areas where they need more practice. This personalized approach not only increases motivation but also ensures that employees acquire the necessary skills and knowledge effectively. By providing a sense of autonomy and control over their learning journey, VR empowers employees and enhances their engagement with the training material.

3.2.3 Emotional Engagement and Empathy

VR has the unique ability to evoke emotional engagement and empathy in learners. By immersing employees in realistic scenarios, VR training can elicit emotional responses that are difficult to replicate with traditional training methods. For example, in customer service training, employees can interact with virtual customers and experience the emotions associated with different customer interactions.

This emotional engagement not only enhances motivation but also improves knowledge retention. Studies have shown that emotional experiences are more likely to be remembered and recalled later. By creating emotional connections with the training material, VR helps employees retain information and apply it effectively in real-world situations.

3.2.4 Gamification and Rewards

Gamification is a powerful technique that can be used to increase motivation and engagement in VR training. By incorporating game elements, such as challenges, rewards, and leaderboards, VR training can transform the learning experience into a fun and interactive game. This gamified approach motivates employees to actively participate and strive for better performance.

Through rewards and recognition, VR training can further enhance motivation and retention. By providing immediate feedback and acknowledging employees' achievements, VR training reinforces positive behaviors and encourages continuous learning. This feedback loop not only boosts motivation but also helps employees track their progress and identify areas for improvement.

3.2.5 Continuous Learning and Reinforcement

VR training offers the opportunity for continuous learning and reinforcement, which is crucial for long-term knowledge retention. Traditional training methods often rely on one-time sessions or periodic workshops, which may not be sufficient to ensure that employees retain the information over time. In contrast, VR training can be easily accessed and revisited whenever needed.

By providing on-demand access to training modules, VR enables employees to refresh their knowledge and skills at their convenience. This continuous learning approach ensures that employees stay engaged and retain the information for longer periods. Additionally, VR training can incorporate spaced repetition techniques, which have been shown to enhance long-term memory retention.

In conclusion, VR has the potential to significantly increase motivation and retention in corporate training. By creating engaging and memorable experiences, offering personalized learning, evoking emotional engagement, incorporating gamification, and enabling continuous learning, VR training can transform the way employees acquire and retain knowledge. HR managers can leverage the power of VR to create impactful training programs that not only enhance employee engagement but also drive better performance and results.

3.3 Improving Skills Acquisition and Application

Virtual Reality (VR) has revolutionized corporate training by providing a highly immersive and interactive learning experience. In this section, we will explore how VR can significantly improve skills acquisition and application in the workplace.

Enhancing Skill Acquisition

Traditional training methods often rely on lectures, presentations, and written materials, which can be passive and less engaging for learners. VR, on the other hand, offers a dynamic and experiential learning environment that actively involves employees in the training process.

By simulating real-world scenarios, VR allows employees to practice and develop their skills in a safe and controlled environment. For example, in industries such as healthcare and manufacturing, VR can provide realistic simulations of medical procedures or equipment operation, allowing employees to gain hands-on experience without the risk of making mistakes.

The immersive nature of VR also enhances the learning experience by stimulating multiple senses. By engaging both visual and auditory senses, VR can improve information retention and recall. Studies have shown that learners who experience training in VR retain information better compared to traditional methods.

Applying Skills in Real-World Situations

One of the key advantages of VR in corporate training is its ability to bridge the gap between theory and practice. After acquiring new skills in a virtual environment, employees can apply them directly to real-world situations.

VR simulations can replicate complex and challenging scenarios that employees may encounter in their job roles. By practicing in these virtual environments, employees can develop the confidence and competence needed to handle similar situations in the workplace.

For example, in customer service training, VR can simulate various customer interactions, allowing employees to practice their communication and problem-solving skills. By providing immediate feedback and guidance, VR enables employees to refine their skills and make adjustments in real-time.

Personalized and Adaptive Learning

VR technology also enables personalized and adaptive learning experiences. Through data tracking and analysis, VR systems can identify individual learning needs and tailor the training content accordingly.

By adapting the difficulty level and content based on the learner's performance, VR ensures that employees are challenged at an appropriate level.

This personalized approach not only enhances engagement but also maximizes the effectiveness of the training.

Additionally, VR can provide real-time performance metrics and analytics, allowing employees and trainers to monitor progress and identify areas for improvement. This feedback loop promotes continuous learning and skill development.

Collaboration and Teamwork

In addition to individual skill acquisition, VR can also foster collaboration and teamwork among employees. Virtual environments can be designed to facilitate group activities and simulations, allowing employees to work together towards a common goal.

By immersing employees in a shared virtual space, VR promotes communication, cooperation, and problem-solving skills. Team members can interact and collaborate in real-time, regardless of their physical location. This is particularly beneficial for organizations with geographically dispersed teams or remote workers.

Furthermore, VR can simulate realistic team-based scenarios, such as crisis management or project planning, where employees can practice their teamwork skills in a risk-free environment. By experiencing these scenarios together, employees can develop a shared understanding and build stronger working relationships.

Conclusion

Virtual Reality has the potential to revolutionize skills acquisition and application in corporate training. By providing immersive and interactive learning experiences, VR enhances employee engagement, retention, and application of skills. The ability to personalize training content and foster collaboration further amplifies the benefits of VR in the workplace. As organizations continue to embrace VR technology, they can unlock the full potential of their workforce and drive innovation and success.

3.4 Fostering Collaboration and Teamwork

Collaboration and teamwork are essential components of a successful corporate training program. In traditional training methods, employees often work individually or in small groups, limiting the opportunities for collaboration and interaction. However, with the introduction of virtual reality (VR) in corporate training, organizations can now create immersive and interactive experiences that foster collaboration and teamwork among employees.

3.4.1 Enhancing Communication and Collaboration

One of the key advantages of VR in corporate training is its ability to simulate real-world scenarios and facilitate communication and collaboration among employees. VR environments can be designed to replicate the workplace, allowing employees to interact with each other and work together on tasks and projects. For example, in a VR training program for project management, employees can collaborate on a virtual project, assigning tasks, sharing information, and communicating in real-time.

By providing a shared virtual space, VR training programs enable employees to collaborate regardless of their physical location. This is particularly beneficial for organizations with remote or distributed teams, as it eliminates the barriers of distance and allows employees to work together seamlessly. VR also provides a sense of presence and immersion, making the collaboration experience more engaging and effective.

3.4.2 Team Building and Problem Solving

VR can also be used to facilitate team building activities and enhance problem-solving skills. In a VR training program focused on team building, employees can participate in virtual team-building exercises and challenges. These exercises can range from solving puzzles and completing tasks together to engaging in virtual team-building games and simulations.

By immersing employees in a virtual environment, VR training programs create a sense of shared experience and promote teamwork. Employees can learn to communicate effectively, delegate tasks, and work together to overcome challenges. This not only enhances their collaboration skills but also strengthens the bonds between team members.

3.4.3 Simulating Real-World Collaboration

VR can simulate real-world collaboration scenarios, allowing employees to practice and refine their collaboration skills in a safe and controlled environment. For example, in a VR training program for sales teams, employees can engage in virtual sales meetings and negotiations with simulated clients. They can practice active listening, effective communication, and collaborative problem-solving techniques.

By providing realistic and immersive simulations, VR training programs enable employees to experience the challenges and dynamics of real-world collaboration. They can learn from their mistakes, receive immediate feedback, and develop the skills necessary for successful collaboration.

3.4.4 Virtual Team Projects

Another way VR can foster collaboration and teamwork is through virtual team projects. In a VR training program, employees can be assigned to virtual teams and work together on complex projects or simulations. These projects can involve multiple departments or functions, requiring employees to collaborate and coordinate their efforts.

Virtual team projects provide employees with the opportunity to develop their teamwork and collaboration skills in a dynamic and interactive environment. They can learn to leverage each other's strengths, communicate effectively, and work towards a common goal. VR training programs can also incorporate gamification elements, such as leaderboards and rewards, to further motivate and engage employees in the collaborative process.

3.4.5 Benefits of Collaborative VR Training

The use of VR in collaborative training offers several benefits for organizations. Firstly, it promotes a sense of belonging and camaraderie among employees, fostering a positive and collaborative work culture. Employees feel more connected to their colleagues and are more likely to collaborate and support each other in their day-to-day work.

Secondly, collaborative VR training enhances employee engagement and motivation. The interactive and immersive nature of VR experiences captivates employees' attention and makes the learning process more enjoyable. When employees are actively engaged in the training, they are more likely to retain information and apply it in their work.

Lastly, collaborative VR training improves the transfer of learning to the workplace. By providing employees with opportunities to practice collaboration and teamwork in a realistic virtual environment, they can develop the skills and confidence necessary to apply them in their job roles. This leads to improved performance and productivity in the workplace.

In conclusion, VR has the potential to revolutionize corporate training by fostering collaboration and teamwork among employees. By creating immersive and interactive experiences, organizations can enhance communication, promote team building, and simulate real-world collaboration scenarios. The benefits of collaborative VR training include improved employee engagement, enhanced problem-solving skills, and increased transfer of learning to the workplace. As organizations continue to embrace VR in their training strategies, the importance of fostering collaboration and teamwork will become even more evident.

Implementing VR in HR Strategies

4.1 Assessing Training Needs and Objectives

Before implementing virtual reality (VR) in corporate training, it is crucial to assess the training needs and objectives of the organization. This assessment will help HR managers determine how VR can best be utilized to enhance the learning experience and achieve the desired outcomes. In this section, we will explore the key steps involved in assessing training needs and objectives for VR implementation.

4.1.1 Identifying Training Gaps

The first step in assessing training needs is to identify any existing gaps in the organization's current training programs. This can be done through various methods such as conducting surveys, interviews, and focus groups with employees and managers. By gathering feedback from key stakeholders, HR managers can gain insights into the specific areas where training is lacking or could be improved.

Additionally, analyzing performance data and conducting skills assessments can provide valuable information about the skills and knowledge gaps within the workforce. This data-driven approach can help HR managers prioritize the areas where VR training can have the greatest impact.

4.1.2 Defining Learning Objectives

Once the training gaps have been identified, the next step is to define clear and measurable learning objectives for the VR training program. Learning objectives outline what employees should be able to do or know after completing the training. These objectives should be aligned with the overall goals and objectives of the organization.

When defining learning objectives, it is important to consider the specific skills and knowledge that need to be developed, as well as any behavioral changes that are desired. For example, if the objective is to improve customer service skills, the VR training program may focus on enhancing communication, problem-solving, and empathy skills.

4.1.3 Analyzing Training Content

After defining the learning objectives, HR managers need to analyze the existing training content to determine what can be effectively delivered through VR. Not all training content is suitable for VR, and it is important to identify the topics and scenarios that can benefit the most from an immersive learning experience.

During this analysis, HR managers should consider the complexity of the content, the level of interactivity required, and the potential for real-world application. VR is particularly effective for training that involves hands-on practice, simulations, and scenarios that are difficult or costly to replicate in traditional training methods.

4.1.4 Assessing Technical Requirements

Another important aspect of assessing training needs and objectives is evaluating the technical requirements for implementing VR training. This includes considering the hardware and software needed to deliver the training, as well as the infrastructure and support systems required.

HR managers should assess the organization's current technological capabilities and determine if any upgrades or investments are necessary. Factors to consider include the availability of VR headsets, the computing power required, and the compatibility with existing systems and platforms.

4.1.5 Considering Learner Preferences and Accessibility

When assessing training needs and objectives, it is essential to consider the preferences and accessibility of the learners. Not all employees may be comfortable or familiar with VR technology, and it is important to address any potential barriers or concerns.

HR managers should gather feedback from employees regarding their willingness to engage with VR training and any specific needs or accommodations that may be required. This information can help shape the design and delivery of the VR training program to ensure maximum engagement and accessibility for all learners.

4.1.6 Developing a Training Plan

Based on the assessment of training needs and objectives, HR managers can develop a comprehensive training plan for implementing VR. This plan should outline the specific training modules, the timeline for implementation, and the resources required.

The training plan should also include a strategy for evaluating the effectiveness of the VR training program. This may involve conducting pre and post-training assessments, gathering feedback from learners, and analyzing performance data to measure the impact of the training on employee skills and performance.

By carefully assessing training needs and objectives, HR managers can ensure that the implementation of VR in corporate training is aligned with the organization's goals and delivers tangible benefits. This assessment process sets the foundation for designing and implementing effective VR training programs that enhance employee engagement, motivation, and performance.

4.2 Designing VR Training Programs

Designing effective virtual reality (VR) training programs is crucial for maximizing the benefits of this immersive learning technology. In this section, we will explore the key considerations and steps involved in designing VR training programs that are engaging, impactful, and aligned with the organization's training objectives.

4.2.1 Identifying Training Needs and Objectives

Before diving into the design process, it is essential to identify the specific training needs and objectives that VR can address. This involves conducting a thorough analysis of the skills and knowledge gaps within the organization and determining how VR can bridge those gaps effectively.

To identify training needs, HR managers can collaborate with subject matter experts, department heads, and employees to understand the areas where traditional training methods may be falling short. By gathering feedback and conducting assessments, HR managers can pinpoint the specific skills or tasks that can benefit from VR training.

Once the training needs are identified, clear and measurable objectives should be established. These objectives should outline what employees should be able to achieve or demonstrate after completing the VR training program. For example, objectives could include improving customer service skills, enhancing decision-making abilities, or increasing safety awareness.

4.2.2 Designing Engaging and Interactive VR Experiences

Designing engaging and interactive VR experiences is crucial for capturing learners' attention and maximizing the effectiveness of the training program. Here are some key considerations when designing VR training programs:

4.2.2.1 Storytelling and Scenario-Based Learning

One of the strengths of VR is its ability to create immersive and realistic scenarios. By incorporating storytelling elements and scenario-based learning, HR managers can enhance the learning experience and make it more relatable to real-world situations. Learners can be placed in virtual environments that simulate workplace challenges, allowing them to practice and apply their skills in a safe and controlled setting.

4.2.2.2 Interactivity and Decision-Making

Interactivity is a crucial aspect of VR training programs. By providing learners with opportunities to make decisions and interact with the virtual environment, HR managers can foster active learning and critical thinking. This can be achieved through interactive simulations, role-playing exercises, and branching scenarios that adapt to learners' choices.

4.2.2.3 Feedback and Assessment

Providing timely and constructive feedback is essential for learners to gauge their progress and improve their performance. In VR training programs, HR managers can incorporate feedback mechanisms such as virtual coaches, performance metrics, and debriefing sessions. These feedback mechanisms can help learners understand their strengths and areas for improvement, ultimately enhancing the learning experience.

4.2.3 Customizing VR Training Content

To ensure the effectiveness of VR training programs, it is crucial to customize the content to meet the specific needs of the organization and its employees. Here are some considerations when customizing VR training content:

4.2.3.1 Tailoring Content to Job Roles and Skill Levels

Different job roles within the organization may require different training content. HR managers should work closely with subject matter experts to identify the specific skills and knowledge that are relevant to each job role. By tailoring the content to job roles and skill levels, HR managers can ensure that the VR training program is targeted and impactful.

4.2.3.2 Incorporating Real-World Scenarios

To make the VR training program more relevant and practical, it is essential to incorporate real-world scenarios that employees are likely to encounter in their roles. By simulating these scenarios in the virtual environment, learners can practice and apply their skills in a context that closely resembles their actual work environment.

4.2.3.3 Adapting Content for Different Learning Styles

People have different learning styles, and VR training programs should cater to these individual preferences. HR managers can consider incorporating different modes of learning, such as visual, auditory, and kinesthetic, to accommodate diverse learning styles. This can be achieved using multimedia elements, interactive exercises, and hands-on simulations.

4.2.4 Piloting and Iterating the VR Training Program

Before rolling out the VR training program organization-wide, it is advisable to conduct a pilot phase to gather feedback and make necessary improvements. During the pilot phase, a small group of employees can participate in the VR training program and provide feedback on its effectiveness, usability, and relevance.

Based on the feedback received, HR managers can iterate and refine the VR training program to address any identified issues or areas for improvement. This iterative process ensures that the final version of the VR training program is well-designed, engaging, and aligned with the organization's training objectives.

By following these steps and considerations, HR managers can design VR training programs that leverage the immersive and interactive nature of virtual reality to enhance employee learning and performance. The next section will explore how to integrate VR into existing training methods to create blended learning experiences.

4.3 Integrating VR into Existing Training Methods

Virtual Reality (VR) has emerged as a powerful tool for corporate training, offering immersive and interactive experiences that can enhance learning outcomes. As organizations look to incorporate VR into their training strategies, it is important to consider how this technology can be integrated into existing training methods. This section will explore various approaches and considerations for integrating VR into traditional training methods.

4.3.1 Blended Learning Approach

One effective way to integrate VR into existing training methods is through a blended learning approach. Blended learning combines traditional classroom instruction with online and interactive elements, and VR can be seamlessly incorporated into this mix. By using VR as a supplement to traditional training methods, organizations can provide learners with a more engaging and immersive experience.

For example, instead of conducting a full training session in a physical classroom, organizations can use VR to simulate real-life scenarios and allow learners to practice their skills in a safe and controlled environment. This can be followed by a debriefing session in the classroom, where learners can discuss their experiences and receive feedback from instructors.

4.3.2 Augmenting Existing Training Materials

Another approach to integrating VR into existing training methods is by augmenting existing training materials with VR content. Organizations can leverage VR technology to enhance traditional training materials such as manuals, videos, and presentations. By adding interactive and immersive elements to these materials, learners can have a more engaging and memorable learning experience.

For instance, instead of watching a video demonstration of a complex process, learners can use VR to virtually experience and interact with the process in a realistic and hands-on manner. This not only improves knowledge retention but also allows learners to develop practical skills through experiential learning.

4.3.3 Virtual Reality Simulations

One of the most powerful applications of VR in training is the ability to create realistic simulations. Organizations can integrate VR simulations into existing training methods to provide learners with a safe and controlled environment to practice and refine their skills.

For example, in industries such as healthcare or manufacturing, where hands-on training is crucial, VR simulations can replicate real-life scenarios and allow learners to perform tasks and make decisions in a virtual environment. This not only reduces the risk of errors and accidents but also provides learners with the opportunity to gain practical experience before working in the actual setting.

4.3.4 Gamification and VR

Gamification is a popular approach to engage learners and motivate them to actively participate in training activities. By combining VR with gamification elements, organizations can create immersive and interactive training experiences that are both enjoyable and effective.

For instance, organizations can develop VR-based training games where learners can compete with each other or earn points and rewards for completing tasks or achieving specific learning objectives. This not only makes the training experience more engaging but also encourages learners to actively participate and apply their knowledge and skills in a competitive and fun environment.

4.3.5 Customizing VR Training for Specific Needs

When integrating VR into existing training methods, it is important to customize the VR training programs to meet the specific needs and objectives of the organization. This involves identifying the key learning outcomes, designing relevant VR scenarios, and aligning the VR training with the overall training strategy.

For example, if the organization aims to improve customer service skills, the VR training program can be designed to simulate various customer interactions and provide learners with the opportunity to practice their communication and problem-solving skills. By customizing the VR training to address specific training needs, organizations can maximize the effectiveness of the training and ensure that learners acquire the desired skills and knowledge.

4.3.6 Integration Challenges and Considerations

While integrating VR into existing training methods offers numerous benefits, there are also challenges and considerations that organizations need to address. These include the cost of VR hardware and software, the need for technical support and maintenance, and the potential resistance from employees who may be unfamiliar or uncomfortable with VR technology.

To overcome these challenges, organizations should carefully plan and budget for the implementation of VR training, provide adequate training and support for employees, and communicate the value and benefits of VR training to gain buy-in from stakeholders. Additionally, organizations should continuously evaluate the effectiveness of the VR training programs and make necessary adjustments to ensure optimal outcomes.

In conclusion, integrating VR into existing training methods can revolutionize corporate training by providing learners with immersive and interactive experiences. By adopting a blended learning approach, augmenting existing training materials, using VR simulations, incorporating gamification elements, customizing VR training, and addressing integration challenges, organizations can effectively leverage VR technology to enhance their training programs and improve employee performance and engagement.

4.4 Measuring the Effectiveness of VR Training

Measuring the effectiveness of any training program is crucial for organizations to determine the return on investment and make informed decisions about its future implementation. Virtual reality (VR) training is no exception. In this section, we will explore various methods and metrics that can be used to evaluate the effectiveness of VR training in a corporate setting.

4.4.1 Key Performance Indicators (KPIs)

To measure the effectiveness of VR training, it is essential to identify and track key performance indicators (KPIs) that align with the training objectives and desired outcomes. KPIs provide measurable data that can be used to assess the impact of VR training on employee performance and engagement. Here are some common KPIs that can be used to evaluate VR training effectiveness:

Knowledge Acquisition: Assessing the extent to which employees have gained new knowledge and understanding through VR training. This can be measured through pre and post-training assessments or quizzes.

Skills Development: Evaluating the improvement in employees' skills and competencies as a result of VR training. This can be measured through performance evaluations, simulations, or practical assessments.

Retention and Transfer: Determining the extent to which employees retain and apply the knowledge and skills learned in VR training to their job tasks. This can be measured through on-the-job observations, supervisor feedback, or follow-up assessments.

Engagement and Motivation: Assessing the level of employee engagement and motivation during VR training sessions. This can be measured through surveys, feedback forms, or self-assessment tools.

Time and Cost Savings: Measuring the efficiency and cost-effectiveness of VR training compared to traditional training methods. This can be evaluated by comparing the time taken to complete training, the cost of training materials, and the reduction in errors or accidents.

User Satisfaction: Gathering feedback from employees about their overall satisfaction with the VR training experience. This can be measured through post-training surveys or interviews.

4.4.2 Data Collection Methods

To collect data for evaluating the effectiveness of VR training, organizations can employ various methods depending on the specific KPIs and objectives. Here are some commonly used data collection methods:

Pre and Post-Training Assessments: Administering assessments or quizzes before and after VR training to measure the knowledge gained or skills developed.

Performance Evaluations: Conducting performance evaluations or observations to assess the application of VR training in real work scenarios.

Surveys and Feedback Forms: Distributing surveys or feedback forms to gather employees' perceptions and experiences of VR training.

Simulations and Practical Assessments: Using simulations or practical assessments to evaluate employees' skills and competencies in a controlled environment.

Usage Analytics: Tracking and analyzing data on the usage of VR training modules, including the time spent, completion rates, and user interactions.

Supervisor Feedback: Seeking feedback from supervisors or managers on the performance improvements or changes observed in employees after VR training.

4.4.3 Data Analysis and Reporting

Once the data has been collected, it is essential to analyze and interpret the results to gain insights into the effectiveness of VR training. Data analysis can involve statistical techniques, such as comparing pre and post-training scores, calculating averages, or conducting correlation analyses. The results can then be presented in a comprehensive report that highlights the impact of VR training on the identified KPIs.

The report should include a summary of the findings, key observations, and recommendations for further improvement. It is crucial to communicate the results effectively to stakeholders, including HR managers, training professionals, and senior leadership, to demonstrate the value and impact of VR training on employee performance and engagement.

4.4.4 Continuous Improvement and Iteration

Measuring the effectiveness of VR training is not a one-time activity but an ongoing process. Organizations should continuously monitor and evaluate the training program to identify areas for improvement and make necessary adjustments. This can involve collecting feedback from employees, conducting follow-up assessments, or analyzing usage analytics to identify patterns or trends.

By continuously measuring and improving the effectiveness of VR training, organizations can ensure that their investment in this technology is delivering the desired outcomes and driving employee performance and engagement.

In the next chapter, we will explore how organizations can identify VR training opportunities and select appropriate content for their training programs.

Building Your VR Training Program

5.1 Identifying VR Training Opportunities

Virtual Reality (VR) has emerged as a powerful tool in the field of corporate training, revolutionizing the way organizations educate and develop their employees. By creating immersive and interactive learning experiences, VR has the potential to enhance employee engagement, improve knowledge retention, and foster practical skills acquisition. However, before implementing a VR training program, it is crucial for HR managers to identify the specific training opportunities where VR can make the most impact.

5.1.1 Assessing Training Needs and Objectives

The first step in identifying VR training opportunities is to assess the training needs and objectives of the organization. This involves understanding the skills and knowledge gaps that exist within the workforce and determining the areas where VR can effectively address these gaps. HR managers should collaborate with department heads, subject matter experts, and employees themselves to gather insights and identify the key training areas that can benefit from VR.

During the assessment process, it is important to consider the complexity and practicality of the training content. VR is particularly effective in simulating real-world scenarios and providing hands-on training experiences. Therefore, training areas that involve complex procedures, high-risk environments, or require practical application of skills are ideal candidates for VR implementation. Additionally, HR managers should consider the scalability and cost-effectiveness of VR training. While VR can provide immersive and engaging experiences, it may not be suitable for every training need. Evaluating the cost of VR hardware, software, and content development, as well as the potential return on investment, is essential in determining the feasibility of implementing VR in specific training areas.

5.1.2 Identifying Training Areas with High Impact

Once the training needs and objectives have been assessed, HR managers can identify the specific training areas where VR can have a high impact. Some common training areas that can benefit from VR include:

Technical Skills Training

VR can be used to train employees on technical skills that require hands-on practice, such as equipment operation, machinery maintenance, or software usage. By creating realistic simulations, VR enables employees to practice and refine their skills in a safe and controlled environment, without the risk of damaging equipment or causing accidents.

Safety Training

Safety training is another area where VR can be highly effective. VR simulations can recreate hazardous situations, such as fire emergencies or workplace accidents, allowing employees to experience and learn how to respond in a safe and controlled environment. This immersive approach to safety training can significantly improve employee preparedness and reduce the risk of workplace incidents.

Soft Skills Development

VR is not limited to technical training; it can also be used to develop essential soft skills, such as communication, leadership, and customer service. Through interactive scenarios and role-playing exercises, VR can provide employees with realistic situations to practice and improve their interpersonal skills. This immersive approach to soft skills training allows employees to receive immediate feedback and learn from their experiences in a risk-free environment.

Onboarding and Orientation

VR can enhance the onboarding and orientation process for new employees by providing them with a virtual tour of the workplace, introducing key personnel, and familiarizing them with company policies and procedures. This immersive experience can help new employees feel more connected to the organization from the start and accelerate their integration into the company culture.

Sales and Customer Service Training

For organizations that rely heavily on sales and customer service, VR can be a valuable tool for training employees in these areas. VR simulations can recreate realistic sales scenarios or customer interactions, allowing employees to practice their sales techniques, product knowledge, and customer service skills. This immersive training approach can help employees build confidence and improve their performance in real-world situations.

5.1.3 Collaboration and Teamwork Training

In addition to individual training, VR can also be used to foster collaboration and teamwork among employees. By creating virtual environments where employees can work together on projects or solve problems, VR can simulate real-world team dynamics and promote effective communication, cooperation, and problem-solving skills. This collaborative training approach can be particularly beneficial for remote teams or geographically dispersed organizations.

5.1.4 Customizing VR Training Content

Once the training areas with high impact have been identified, HR managers can start customizing the VR training content to meet the specific needs of the organization. This involves working closely with VR content developers or external vendors to create tailored training scenarios and simulations that align with the organization's objectives and desired learning outcomes.

It is important to ensure that the VR training content is engaging, interactive, and relevant to the target audience. By incorporating gamification elements, interactive quizzes, and branching scenarios, HR managers can enhance the learning experience and increase employee engagement. Regularly updating and refreshing the VR training content is also crucial to keep employees motivated and prevent training fatigue.

In conclusion, identifying VR training opportunities requires a thorough assessment of training needs and objectives, as well as a careful evaluation of the areas where VR can have the most impact. By focusing on technical skills training, safety training, soft skills development, onboarding and orientation, sales and customer service training, and collaboration and teamwork training, HR managers can leverage the power of VR to transform corporate training and unlock the full potential of their employees.

5.2 Selecting VR Training Content

When implementing a virtual reality (VR) training program, one of the crucial steps is selecting the appropriate content. The content you choose will determine the effectiveness of the training and the overall impact it has on your employees. In this section, we will explore the key considerations and best practices for selecting VR training content.

5.2.1 Identifying Training Needs and Objectives

Before selecting VR training content, it is essential to identify the specific training needs and objectives of your organization. This involves understanding the skills and knowledge gaps that need to be addressed and determining the desired outcomes of the training program. By clearly defining your training goals, you can align the VR content with your organization's needs and ensure that it delivers the desired results.

To identify training needs and objectives, consider conducting a thorough training needs analysis. This analysis can involve assessing the current skill levels of your employees, gathering feedback from managers and supervisors, and identifying any performance gaps or areas for improvement. By understanding the specific areas where VR training can make a significant impact, you can focus on developing content that directly addresses those needs.

5.2.2 Customizing Content for Your Organization

Once you have identified the training needs and objectives, the next step is to customize the VR training content to suit your organization's unique requirements. While there may be off-the-shelf VR training solutions available, tailoring the content to your organization's specific context and industry can enhance the effectiveness of the training.

Customizing the content involves incorporating relevant scenarios, tasks, and challenges that closely resemble the real-world situations your employees encounter. By creating a realistic and immersive training experience, you can ensure that the skills and knowledge gained in the virtual environment can be easily transferred to the actual workplace.

Additionally, consider incorporating your organization's branding and culture into the VR training content. This can help create a sense of familiarity and engagement among your employees, making the training more relatable and impactful.

5.2.3 Balancing Realism and Learning Objectives

When selecting VR training content, it is crucial to strike a balance between realism and the learning objectives of the training program. While it is essential to create an immersive and realistic environment, the primary focus should be on achieving the desired learning outcomes.

Ensure that the VR content aligns with the specific skills and knowledge that need to be acquired or improved. This may involve designing scenarios and simulations that replicate real-world challenges and tasks, allowing employees to practice and apply their skills in a safe and controlled environment.

However, be cautious not to prioritize realism at the expense of the learning objectives. Sometimes, overly complex or realistic scenarios can distract learners from the core learning goals. It is essential to strike a balance that provides an engaging and immersive experience while keeping the focus on the desired learning outcomes.

5.2.4 Incorporating Interactivity and Engagement

To maximize the effectiveness of VR training, it is crucial to incorporate interactivity and engagement into the content. VR technology offers unique opportunities for learners to actively participate and engage with the training material, enhancing their learning experience.

Consider incorporating interactive elements such as simulations, quizzes, and decision-making scenarios that require learners to actively engage and make choices. This not only enhances their understanding of the subject matter but also promotes critical thinking and problem-solving skills.

Furthermore, leverage the capabilities of VR technology to create a sense of presence and immersion. This can be achieved through realistic graphics, spatial audio, and haptic feedback, which can significantly enhance the overall engagement and effectiveness of the training.

5.2.5 Adapting Content for Different Learning Styles

People have different learning styles, and it is essential to consider these variations when selecting VR training content. Some individuals may learn best through visual demonstrations, while others may prefer hands-on experiences or auditory instructions.

To accommodate different learning styles, ensure that the VR training content incorporates a variety of instructional methods. This can include visual cues, audio instructions, interactive elements, and opportunities for hands-on practice. By catering to different learning preferences, you can maximize the effectiveness of the training and ensure that all employees can benefit from the VR experience.

5.2.6 Evaluating and Updating Content

Lastly, it is crucial to continuously evaluate and update the VR training content to ensure its relevance and effectiveness. Regularly assess the impact of the training on employee performance and engagement and gather feedback from learners and trainers.

Based on the feedback and evaluation results, make necessary updates and improvements to the content. This can involve refining scenarios, incorporating new technologies or techniques, or addressing any identified gaps or limitations. By continuously improving the content, you can ensure that the VR training program remains effective and aligned with your organization's evolving needs.

In conclusion, selecting VR training content requires careful consideration of training needs, customization, balancing realism and learning objectives, incorporating interactivity and engagement, adapting to different learning styles, and evaluating and updating the content. By following these best practices, you can create a VR training program that effectively addresses your organization's training goals and delivers a transformative learning experience for your employees.

5.3 Creating VR Training Scenarios

Creating effective and engaging virtual reality (VR) training scenarios is a crucial step in building a successful VR training program. VR training scenarios provide learners with immersive and realistic experiences that allow them to practice and apply their skills in a safe and controlled environment. In this section, we will explore the key considerations and best practices for creating VR training scenarios that maximize learning outcomes and engagement.

5.3.1 Identifying Learning Objectives

Before creating VR training scenarios, it is essential to clearly define the learning objectives. These objectives should align with the overall training goals and address specific skills or knowledge that employees need to acquire or improve. By identifying the learning objectives, you can design VR scenarios that effectively target these objectives and provide learners with relevant and meaningful experiences.

To identify the learning objectives, consider the specific tasks or situations that employees will encounter in their roles. For example, if the training program aims to enhance customer service skills, the learning objectives may include improving communication, problem-solving, and empathy. By understanding the desired outcomes, you can design VR scenarios that simulate real-world situations and allow learners to practice and develop these skills.

5.3.2 Designing Realistic and Engaging Scenarios

To create effective VR training scenarios, it is crucial to design realistic and engaging experiences that replicate the challenges and complexities of the real world. The more immersive and authentic the scenarios, the more engaged and motivated learners will be. Here are some key considerations for designing VR training scenarios:

Contextualization: Situate the scenarios within relevant and relatable contexts. For example, if the training focuses on sales techniques, create scenarios that simulate a sales meeting or a customer interaction. By providing a realistic context, learners can better understand the relevance of the training and apply their skills in a meaningful way.

Interactivity: Incorporate interactive elements into the scenarios to promote active learning. Allow learners to make decisions, solve problems, and interact with virtual objects or characters. By providing opportunities for active participation, learners can engage in experiential learning and develop their skills through practice and feedback.

Variety and Complexity: Design scenarios that vary in complexity and challenge level. Start with simpler scenarios to introduce learners to the basic concepts and gradually increase the difficulty as they progress. This progression allows learners to build their skills incrementally and ensures a smooth learning curve.

Real-time Feedback: Provide immediate and constructive feedback to learners during the scenarios. Use visual cues, audio prompts, or virtual characters to guide learners and highlight areas for improvement. Real-time feedback helps learners understand their strengths and weaknesses and encourages continuous learning and improvement.

Branching Scenarios: Incorporate branching scenarios that offer multiple paths and outcomes based on learners' decisions. This approach allows learners to explore different options and consequences, promoting critical thinking and decision-making skills. Branching scenarios also increase engagement and replayability, as learners can experience different outcomes and learn from their choices.

5.3.3 Collaboration and Social Learning

VR training scenarios can also be designed to foster collaboration and social learning. By incorporating multiplayer features, learners can interact and collaborate with their peers in the virtual environment. This collaborative learning approach promotes teamwork, communication, and problem-solving skills, which are essential in many workplace settings.

Consider designing scenarios that require learners to work together to solve a problem or achieve a common goal. This collaborative element not only enhances the learning experience but also provides an opportunity for learners to practice and develop their interpersonal skills.

5.3.4 Iterative Design and Evaluation

Creating VR training scenarios is an iterative process that involves continuous design, testing, and evaluation. It is essential to gather feedback from learners and subject matter experts throughout the development process to ensure that the scenarios meet the intended learning objectives and engage the learners effectively.

Conduct pilot tests with a small group of learners to gather feedback on the scenarios' usability, realism, and effectiveness. Use this feedback to refine and improve the scenarios before deploying them on a larger scale. Regular evaluation and refinement of the VR training scenarios will help optimize the learning experience and ensure that the training program delivers the desired outcomes.

By following these best practices and considering the unique characteristics of VR technology, you can create immersive and impactful training scenarios that enhance learning outcomes and engage employees in a whole new way. The next section will explore the implementation of VR training infrastructure, providing guidance on the technical requirements and considerations for setting up a VR training program within your organization.

5.4 Implementing VR Training Infrastructure

Implementing a virtual reality (VR) training program requires careful planning and consideration of various factors. In this section, we will explore the key steps involved in setting up the infrastructure for VR training within your organization.

5.4.1 Assessing Technical Requirements

Before implementing VR training, it is essential to assess the technical requirements of your organization. This includes evaluating the hardware and software needed to support VR experiences. Consider the following factors:

5.4.1.1 Hardware

Evaluate the hardware requirements for VR training, including the VR headsets, controllers, and tracking systems. Determine the number of devices needed based on the size of your training program and the number of employees who will be participating simultaneously. Consider factors such as comfort, ease of use, and compatibility with existing systems.

5.4.1.2 Software

Select the appropriate VR software that aligns with your training objectives. Look for software that offers a wide range of interactive features, realistic simulations, and customization options. Consider whether the software integrates with your existing learning management system (LMS) or if you need to invest in a new platform.

5.4.1.3 Network Infrastructure

Ensure that your organization's network infrastructure can support the bandwidth requirements of VR training. VR experiences often require high-speed internet connections to deliver seamless and immersive training. Assess your network capacity and consider any necessary upgrades to ensure a smooth training experience for your employees.

5.4.2 Creating a Dedicated VR Training Space

To maximize the effectiveness of VR training, it is recommended to create a dedicated space within your organization for VR experiences. Consider the following aspects when setting up the VR training space:

5.4.2.1 Physical Space

Evaluate the physical space available for VR training. Ensure that it is large enough to accommodate the VR equipment and allows for free movement of participants. Consider factors such as lighting, ventilation, and safety precautions to create a comfortable and secure environment.

5.4.2.2 Tracking System Setup

Set up the tracking system within the VR training space to enable accurate movement tracking. This may involve installing cameras or sensors to capture the movements of participants and their interactions with the virtual environment. Ensure that the tracking system is properly calibrated and aligned to provide an optimal training experience.

5.4.2.3 Safety Measures

Implement safety measures to protect participants during VR training. This may include providing guidelines on how to use the equipment safely, ensuring proper hygiene practices, and establishing protocols for emergencies or accidents. Consider providing participants with safety equipment such as wrist straps to prevent accidental dropping of VR devices.

5.4.3 Training and Support for Participants

To ensure a successful implementation of VR training, it is crucial to provide adequate training and support for participants. Consider the following aspects:

5.4.3.1 Training Programs

Develop comprehensive training programs to familiarize participants with the VR equipment, software, and training protocols. Provide hands-on training sessions to help participants understand how to navigate the virtual environment, interact with objects, and perform tasks effectively. Offer ongoing support and refresher training as needed.

5.4.3.2 Technical Support

Establish a dedicated technical support team to assist participants with any technical issues they may encounter during VR training. This team should be well-versed in troubleshooting VR hardware and software problems and be readily available to provide prompt assistance. Consider providing participants with a helpdesk or online support portal for easy access to technical support.

5.4.3.3 User Feedback and Evaluation

Encourage participants to provide feedback on their VR training experiences. Regularly evaluate the effectiveness of the training program and make necessary improvements based on user feedback. This feedback loop will help identify any issues or areas for improvement and ensure continuous enhancement of the VR training program.

5.4.4 Integration with Existing Systems

Integrating VR training with your organization's existing systems can streamline the training process and enhance the overall learning experience. Consider the following integration options:

5.4.4.1 Learning Management System (LMS)

Integrate the VR training program with your organization's LMS to track and manage employee training progress. This integration allows for seamless enrollment, progress tracking, and reporting of VR training activities. Ensure that the LMS supports the necessary features and functionalities required for VR training integration.

5.4.4.2 Performance Management Systems

Integrate VR training data with your organization's performance management systems to assess the impact of VR training on employee performance. This integration can provide valuable insights into the effectiveness of the training program and help identify areas for improvement.

5.4.4.3 HR and Talent Management Systems

Consider integrating VR training data with your organization's HR and talent management systems. This integration can help identify skill gaps, track employee development, and align VR training with career progression and succession planning initiatives.

5.4.5 Security and Data Privacy

When implementing VR training infrastructure, it is essential to prioritize security and data privacy. Consider the following measures:

5.4.5.1 Data Protection

Implement robust data protection measures to safeguard sensitive employee data collected during VR training. Ensure compliance with relevant data protection regulations and establish protocols for data storage, access, and retention.

5.4.5.2 User Privacy

Respect user privacy by obtaining informed consent for data collection and usage. Clearly communicate the purpose and scope of data collection and provide participants with options to opt-out if desired. Regularly review and update privacy policies to align with evolving privacy regulations.

5.4.5.3 Cybersecurity

Implement cybersecurity measures to protect VR training infrastructure from potential threats. This includes securing network connections, regularly updating software and firmware, and educating participants about cybersecurity best practices.

Implementing VR training infrastructure requires careful planning, technical assessment, and consideration of various factors. By following the steps outlined in this section, you can create a robust and effective VR training program that enhances employee learning and engagement.

Case Study

Johnson & Johnson

6.1 Overview of Johnson & Johnson's VR Training Program

Johnson & Johnson, a global healthcare company, has been at the forefront of leveraging virtual reality (VR) technology to enhance their corporate training programs. By incorporating VR into their training initiatives, Johnson & Johnson has revolutionized the way their employees learn, practice, and apply critical skills in a safe and immersive environment.

6.1.1 Introduction to Johnson & Johnson's VR Training Program

Johnson & Johnson recognized the potential of VR technology early on and embarked on a journey to integrate it into their training strategies. Their VR training program focuses on various areas, including medical device training, surgical simulations, sales training, and soft skills development.

6.1.2 Key Components of Johnson & Johnson's VR Training Program

6.1.2.1 Medical Device Training

One of the key areas where Johnson & Johnson has successfully implemented VR is in medical device training. Through VR simulations, healthcare professionals can practice using complex medical devices in a realistic and risk-free environment. This immersive training allows them to gain hands-on experience, improve their proficiency, and enhance patient safety.

6.1.2.2 Surgical Simulations

Johnson & Johnson's VR training program also includes surgical simulations, which provide surgeons with a platform to practice and refine their surgical techniques. By replicating real-life surgical scenarios, surgeons can enhance their skills, improve patient outcomes, and reduce the risk of errors during actual surgeries.

6.1.2.3 Sales Training

In addition to medical training, Johnson & Johnson utilizes VR to train their sales representatives. Through interactive VR scenarios, sales professionals can practice their pitch, engage with virtual customers, and develop effective communication and negotiation skills. This immersive training approach enables them to gain confidence and improve their sales performance.

6.1.2.4 Soft Skills Development

Johnson & Johnson recognizes the importance of soft skills in the workplace and has integrated VR into their training programs to develop these skills. Through VR simulations, employees can practice scenarios that require effective communication, teamwork, leadership, and problem-solving. This immersive training helps employees enhance their interpersonal skills and adaptability, leading to improved collaboration and overall performance.

6.1.3 Success Factors and Lessons Learned

Johnson & Johnson's VR training program has achieved remarkable success, and several key factors have contributed to its effectiveness:

6.1.3.1 Immersive and Realistic Simulations

The use of VR technology allows Johnson & Johnson to create highly immersive and realistic training simulations. By replicating real-world scenarios, employees can experience the challenges and complexities they may encounter in their roles. This realism enhances engagement, knowledge retention, and skill acquisition.

6.1.3.2 Personalized and Adaptive Learning

Johnson & Johnson's VR training program offers personalized and adaptive learning experiences. The program can adapt to the individual needs and skill levels of each employee, providing targeted training and feedback. This personalized approach ensures that employees receive the right level of challenge and support, maximizing their learning outcomes.

6.1.3.3 Continuous Feedback and Assessment

VR technology enables Johnson & Johnson to provide immediate feedback and assessment to employees during their training sessions. This real-time feedback allows employees to identify areas for improvement and make adjustments in their performance. The continuous assessment also helps trainers and HR professionals track progress and measure the effectiveness of the training program.

6.1.3.4 Collaboration and Knowledge Sharing

Johnson & Johnson's VR training program promotes collaboration and knowledge sharing among employees. Through multiplayer VR experiences, employees can work together, solve problems, and learn from each other's experiences. This collaborative learning environment fosters teamwork, communication, and a sense of community among employees.

6.1.4 Impact on Employee Performance and Engagement

Johnson & Johnson's VR training program has had a significant impact on employee performance and engagement:

6.1.4.1 Improved Skill Acquisition and Application

The immersive nature of VR training allows employees to acquire and apply skills more effectively. By practicing in realistic scenarios, employees can develop muscle memory, refine techniques, and gain confidence in their abilities. This leads to improved performance and better outcomes in their respective roles.

6.1.4.2 Increased Engagement and Motivation

VR training provides an engaging and interactive learning experience that captures employees' attention and motivates them to actively participate. The immersive nature of VR stimulates multiple senses, making the training more memorable and enjoyable. This increased engagement translates into higher motivation and a willingness to apply learned skills in real-world situations.

6.1.4.3 Enhanced Retention and Transfer of Knowledge

Studies have shown that VR training improves knowledge retention and transfer. The realistic and immersive nature of VR simulations creates strong memory associations, making the learned information more memorable and easier to recall.

Employees are more likely to retain and apply the knowledge gained through VR training in their day-to-day work.

6.1.5 Recommendations for Other Companies

Based on the success of Johnson & Johnson's VR training program, here are some recommendations for other companies looking to implement VR in their corporate training:

Identify specific training needs and objectives that can benefit from VR technology.

Invest in high-quality VR hardware and software to ensure a realistic and immersive training experience.

Collaborate with subject matter experts and instructional designers to create effective VR training content.

Provide ongoing support and resources to employees during their VR training journey.

Continuously evaluate and measure the effectiveness of the VR training program to make necessary improvements.

By following these recommendations, companies can unlock the full potential of VR technology in their corporate training programs and drive positive outcomes for their employees and organizations.

6.2 Success Factors and Lessons Learned

In this section, we will explore the success factors and lessons learned from the implementation of virtual reality (VR) training programs in various companies. By examining the experiences of these organizations, we can gain valuable insights into the key factors that contribute to the success of VR training initiatives and learn from their lessons.

6.2.1 Commitment from Top Management

One of the common success factors among the companies that have implemented VR training programs is the strong commitment from top management. In each case study, we found that the leadership team recognized the potential of VR technology in transforming corporate training and actively supported its implementation. This commitment was demonstrated through the allocation of resources, including budget and personnel, to ensure the success of the VR training programs.

6.2.2 Alignment with Training Objectives

Another critical success factor is the alignment of VR training programs with the organization's training objectives. Companies that achieved significant results with VR training clearly defined their training goals and identified the specific areas where VR could provide the most value. By focusing on these areas, they were able to design immersive and targeted training experiences that directly addressed the identified needs.

6.2.3 Collaboration with Subject Matter Experts

Successful implementation of VR training programs also involved close collaboration with subject matter experts (SMEs). These experts played a crucial role in designing the training content and scenarios, ensuring that they accurately reflected real-world situations and challenges. By involving SMEs from the beginning, the companies were able to create highly realistic and effective training experiences that resonated with the trainees.

6.2.4 Customization and Personalization

Customization and personalization were key factors in the success of VR training programs. Companies that achieved positive outcomes tailored the training content to the specific needs of their employees and the organization. They recognized that one-size-fits-all approaches may not be as effective and instead focused on creating personalized learning experiences that catered to individual learning styles and preferences.

6.2.5 Continuous Evaluation and Improvement

Continuous evaluation and improvement were integral to the success of VR training programs. Companies that achieved the best results regularly assessed the effectiveness of their VR training initiatives and made necessary adjustments based on feedback and data. This iterative approach allowed them to refine the training content, scenarios, and delivery methods, ensuring that the VR training programs remained relevant and impactful.

6.2.6 Integration with Existing Training Methods

Successful companies also recognized the importance of integrating VR training with existing training methods. They understood that VR was not meant to replace traditional training approaches but rather enhance them. By seamlessly integrating VR into their overall training strategies, these companies were able to create a blended learning environment that combined the benefits of both virtual and traditional training methods.

6.2.7 Employee Engagement and Support

Employee engagement and support were crucial factors in the success of VR training programs.

Companies that achieved high levels of employee engagement actively involved their employees in the design and implementation of the VR training initiatives. They provided opportunities for feedback and encouraged open communication, creating a sense of ownership and empowerment among the trainees. Additionally, these companies offered comprehensive support and resources to ensure that employees could fully embrace and benefit from the VR training programs.

6.2.8 Measuring and Demonstrating ROI

Measuring and demonstrating return on investment (ROI) was an important aspect of the success of VR training programs. Companies that were able to showcase the positive impact of VR training on employee performance and engagement gained support and buy-in from stakeholders. They utilized both qualitative and quantitative metrics to evaluate the effectiveness of the VR training programs and presented the results in a compelling manner to highlight the value of their initiatives.

6.2.9 Continuous Learning and Adaptation

Lastly, successful companies embraced a culture of continuous learning and adaptation. They recognized that VR technology and its applications in corporate training were evolving rapidly. Therefore, they encouraged their HR and training professionals to stay updated with the latest trends and innovations in VR training. By fostering a culture of continuous learning and adaptation, these companies were able to stay ahead of the curve and leverage new opportunities to enhance their VR training programs.

By understanding and implementing these success factors, organizations can increase the likelihood of achieving positive outcomes with their VR training initiatives. The lessons learned from these case studies provide valuable guidance for HR managers and training professionals who are considering or already implementing VR in their corporate training programs.

6.3 Impact on Employee Performance and Engagement

Virtual Reality (VR) has revolutionized corporate training by providing immersive and interactive learning experiences. In this section, we will explore the impact of VR on employee performance and engagement. We will examine how VR training programs have enhanced employee skills, increased motivation, and fostered a culture of continuous learning.

6.3.1 Enhancing Skills Acquisition and Application

One of the key benefits of VR in corporate training is its ability to enhance skills acquisition and application. Traditional training methods often rely on theoretical knowledge and passive learning, which may not effectively translate into practical skills. VR, on the other hand, offers a hands-on approach that allows employees to practice and apply their skills in a realistic and immersive environment.

By simulating real-world scenarios, VR training enables employees to develop and refine their skills in a safe and controlled setting. For example, in the healthcare industry, VR can be used to train medical professionals in complex procedures such as surgery or emergency response. By practicing these procedures in a virtual environment, healthcare professionals can gain confidence and proficiency before performing them on real patients.

Furthermore, VR training allows employees to make mistakes without real-world consequences. This promotes a culture of experimentation and learning from failures, which is crucial for skill development. Employees can repeat training modules as many times as needed, reinforcing their learning and improving their performance over time.

6.3.2 Increasing Motivation and Engagement

Traditional training methods often struggle to keep employees engaged and motivated. Lectures and presentations can be monotonous, leading to decreased attention and retention. VR training, on the other hand, offers a highly engaging and interactive experience that captivates employees' attention and motivates them to actively participate in the learning process.

The immersive nature of VR creates a sense of presence, making employees feel as if they are physically present in the training environment. This heightened sense of realism and interactivity stimulates employees' curiosity and encourages them to explore and engage with the training content. As a result, employees are more likely to retain information and apply it effectively in their job roles.

Moreover, VR training can be gamified, incorporating elements of competition, rewards, and challenges. This gamification aspect adds an element of fun and excitement to the training experience, further enhancing employee motivation and engagement. By setting goals, tracking progress, and providing instant feedback, VR training programs create a sense of achievement and accomplishment, driving employees to strive for continuous improvement.

6.3.3 Fostering Collaboration and Teamwork

In addition to enhancing individual performance, VR training also fosters collaboration and teamwork among employees. Virtual environments can be designed to simulate group activities and scenarios, allowing employees to work together and solve problems as a team.

By collaborating in a virtual space, employees can develop essential teamwork skills such as communication, coordination, and decision-making. They can practice working in diverse teams, overcoming challenges, and leveraging each other's strengths. This collaborative learning experience not only enhances employee performance but also strengthens the overall team dynamics within the organization.

Furthermore, VR training can facilitate remote collaboration, enabling employees from different locations to participate in training programs together. This is particularly beneficial for global organizations with geographically dispersed teams. By breaking down geographical barriers, VR training promotes cross-cultural understanding and collaboration, fostering a more inclusive and cohesive work environment.

6.3.4 Measuring the Impact

Measuring the impact of VR training on employee performance and engagement is essential to evaluate the effectiveness of the program and make data-driven decisions. Various metrics can be used to assess the impact, including performance improvement, knowledge retention, and employee satisfaction.

Performance improvement can be measured by comparing employees' performance before and after VR training. Key performance indicators (KPIs) specific to each job role can be tracked to determine the extent to which VR training has contributed to improved performance.

Knowledge retention can be assessed through quizzes or assessments administered before and after the training. By comparing the scores, organizations can determine the effectiveness of VR training in knowledge acquisition and retention.

Employee satisfaction surveys can provide valuable insights into the impact of VR training on engagement and motivation. By gathering feedback from employees, organizations can identify areas of improvement and make necessary adjustments to the training program.

In conclusion, VR training has a significant impact on employee performance and engagement. By enhancing skills acquisition, increasing motivation, and fostering collaboration, VR training programs empower employees to reach their full potential. Organizations that embrace VR in their training strategies are likely to see improved employee performance, higher job satisfaction, and a competitive edge in the market.

Case study

Chevron

7.1 Overview of Chevron's VR Training Program

Chevron, one of the world's leading energy companies, has embraced the power of virtual reality (VR) in its corporate training programs. By leveraging immersive technology, Chevron has revolutionized the way it trains its employees, enhancing their learning experience and improving their performance. In this section, we will explore the key aspects of Chevron's VR training program, including its objectives, implementation strategies, and the impact it has had on employee performance and engagement.

7.1.1 Objectives of Chevron's VR Training Program

Chevron's VR training program was designed with specific objectives in mind. The company aimed to provide its employees with a realistic and interactive learning environment that would enable them to acquire and apply essential skills more effectively. By leveraging VR technology, Chevron sought to enhance employee engagement, increase knowledge retention, and improve overall performance.

7.1.2 Implementation Strategies

To implement its VR training program, Chevron adopted a systematic approach that involved careful planning, content development, and infrastructure setup. The company collaborated with VR experts and instructional designers to create immersive and engaging training scenarios that closely simulated real-world situations. Chevron also invested in state-of-the-art VR hardware and software to ensure a seamless and immersive training experience for its employees.

Chevron's training program incorporated a variety of VR applications, including simulations of hazardous work environments, equipment operation, and emergency response scenarios. These applications allowed employees to practice their skills in a safe and controlled environment, reducing the risk of accidents and improving their confidence in handling challenging situations.

7.1.3 Impact on Employee Performance and Engagement

Chevron's VR training program has had a significant impact on employee performance and engagement. By providing employees with hands-on experience in realistic scenarios, the program has improved their ability to apply their knowledge and skills in real-world situations. This has resulted in increased confidence and competence among employees, leading to enhanced job performance and productivity.

The immersive nature of VR training has also contributed to higher levels of employee engagement. The interactive and engaging nature of the training scenarios has captured employees' attention and motivated them to actively participate in the learning process. This has resulted in improved knowledge retention and a greater willingness to apply what they have learned in their day-to-day work.

7.1.4 Lessons Learned and Success Factors

Chevron's VR training program has been successful due to several key factors. First and foremost, the company recognized the potential of VR technology in enhancing employee training and was willing to invest in the necessary resources. By partnering with VR experts and instructional designers, Chevron was able to create high-quality and effective training content that met the specific needs of its employees.

Another critical success factor was the integration of VR training into Chevron's existing training methods. The company recognized that VR was not meant to replace traditional training methods but rather to complement them. By incorporating VR into a blended learning approach, Chevron was able to provide a comprehensive and well-rounded training experience for its employees.

Furthermore, Chevron's commitment to continuous improvement and evaluation played a crucial role in the success of its VR training program. The company regularly collected feedback from employees and used it to refine and enhance the training content and delivery methods. This iterative approach ensured that the VR training program remained relevant and effective over time.

7.1.5 Recommendations for Other Companies

Based on Chevron's experience, there are several recommendations for other companies looking to implement VR training programs. First, it is essential to conduct a thorough needs assessment to identify the specific training objectives and areas where VR can add value. This will help ensure that the VR training program aligns with the company's overall training strategy and addresses the specific needs of its employees.

Second, companies should invest in high-quality VR hardware and software to provide a seamless and immersive training experience. The technology should be user-friendly and capable of delivering realistic and interactive training scenarios.

Lastly, companies should consider integrating VR training into their existing training methods to create a blended learning approach. This will allow employees to benefit from the strengths of both traditional and VR training methods, resulting in a more comprehensive and effective training experience.

In conclusion, Chevron's VR training program has demonstrated the immense potential of virtual reality in corporate training. By leveraging immersive technology, Chevron has enhanced employee engagement, improved performance, and created a safer and more effective learning environment. Other companies can learn from Chevron's success and leverage VR to transform their own corporate training programs.

7.2 Success Factors and Lessons Learned

In this section, we will explore the success factors and lessons learned from the implementation of virtual reality (VR) training programs in various companies. By examining the experiences of these organizations, we can gain valuable insights into the key factors that contribute to the success of VR training initiatives and learn from their lessons.

7.2.1 Commitment from Leadership

One of the common success factors among the companies that have implemented VR training programs is the commitment from leadership. In each case study, we found that the top management of these organizations recognized the potential of VR in transforming corporate training and actively supported its implementation. This commitment was evident in the allocation of resources, including budget and personnel, to ensure the success of the VR training programs.

7.2.2 Alignment with Training Objectives

Another critical success factor is the alignment of VR training programs with the organization's training objectives. Companies that achieved positive outcomes from their VR training initiatives carefully identified the specific skills and knowledge gaps that needed to be addressed. By aligning the VR training content and scenarios with these objectives, they were able to deliver targeted and effective training experiences.

7.2.3 Customization and Tailoring

Successful VR training programs were often customized and tailored to meet the unique needs of the organizations and their employees. These companies recognized that a one-size-fits-all approach would not yield optimal results. Instead, they invested time and effort in designing VR training experiences that were relevant, engaging, and specific to the roles and responsibilities of their employees.

7.2.4 Integration with Existing Training Methods

Integrating VR training with existing training methods was another success factor observed in the case studies. Companies that effectively integrated

VR into their training programs recognized the value of blending traditional training approaches with immersive VR experiences. By combining VR with other training methods such as classroom instruction, e-learning modules, and on-the-job training, these organizations were able to create a comprehensive and well-rounded training curriculum.

7.2.5 User-Centric Design

User-centric design played a crucial role in the success of VR training programs. The companies that achieved positive outcomes focused on creating intuitive and user-friendly VR training experiences. They prioritized the needs and preferences of the learners, ensuring that the VR simulations were easy to navigate, interactive, and provided immediate feedback. By placing the user at the center of the design process, these organizations were able to enhance engagement and learning outcomes.

7.2.6 Continuous Evaluation and Improvement

Continuous evaluation and improvement were key factors in the success of VR training programs. The companies that achieved the best results regularly assessed the effectiveness of their VR training initiatives and made necessary adjustments based on feedback and data. They actively sought input from employees and trainers to identify areas for improvement and implemented changes to enhance the training experience continually.

7.2.7 Employee Engagement and Support

Employee engagement and support were critical to the success of VR training programs. The companies that achieved high levels of employee engagement actively involved their workforce in the design and implementation of VR training initiatives. They provided comprehensive training and support to ensure that employees were comfortable and confident in using VR technology. By fostering a culture of support and enthusiasm, these organizations created an environment where employees embraced VR training as a valuable learning tool.

7.2.8 Measuring and Demonstrating ROI

Measuring and demonstrating return on investment (ROI) was an important success factor for the companies that implemented VR training programs. These organizations recognized the need to quantify the impact of VR training on employee performance and engagement. By collecting data and analyzing key metrics, such as improved skill acquisition, increased productivity, and reduced training costs, they were able to demonstrate the tangible benefits of VR training to stakeholders and secure ongoing support for their initiatives.

7.2.9 Scalability and Sustainability

Scalability and sustainability were crucial considerations for the successful implementation of VR training programs. The companies that achieved long-term success with VR training ensured that their initiatives could be scaled up to accommodate a growing number of employees and training needs. They also established processes and systems to support the ongoing maintenance and updates of VR training content, ensuring its relevance and effectiveness over time.

7.2.10 Collaboration and Knowledge Sharing

Collaboration and knowledge sharing were common themes among the companies that successfully implemented VR training programs.

These organizations recognized the value of sharing best practices, lessons learned, and success stories with other departments and external stakeholders. By fostering a culture of collaboration and knowledge exchange, they were able to accelerate the adoption of VR training and inspire others to explore its potential in their respective organizations.

By examining these success factors and lessons learned from the case studies, HR managers can gain valuable insights into the key considerations and strategies for implementing VR training programs in their own organizations. These insights can guide them in designing and implementing effective VR training initiatives that enhance employee engagement, improve performance, and drive organizational success.

7.3 Impact on Employee Performance and Engagement

Virtual reality (VR) has revolutionized corporate training by providing immersive and interactive learning experiences. In this section, we will explore the impact of VR on employee performance and engagement. We will examine how VR enhances learning outcomes, increases motivation and retention, improves skills acquisition and application, and fosters collaboration and teamwork.

7.3.1 Enhancing Learning Outcomes

One of the key benefits of VR in corporate training is its ability to enhance learning outcomes. Traditional training methods often rely on passive learning, where employees passively absorb information without actively engaging with the content. VR, on the other hand, allows employees to actively participate in realistic and interactive scenarios, which leads to better knowledge retention and application.

By immersing employees in virtual environments that replicate real-life situations, VR enables them to practice and apply their skills in a safe and controlled setting. This hands-on approach to learning not only improves knowledge retention but also enhances critical thinking, problem-solving, and decision-making abilities. Employees can learn from their mistakes in a risk-free environment, which boosts their confidence and competence when facing similar challenges in the real world.

7.3.2 Increasing Motivation and Retention

Motivating employees to actively engage in training programs can be a challenge for HR managers. Traditional training methods often fail to capture employees' attention and interest, leading to low motivation and poor retention of information. VR addresses this challenge by providing a highly engaging and immersive learning experience.

The interactive nature of VR training stimulates employees' curiosity and encourages them to explore and experiment. By offering a sense of presence and agency, VR creates a compelling learning environment that captivates employees' attention and motivates them to actively participate in the training. This increased motivation translates into higher retention rates, as employees are more likely to remember and apply the knowledge and skills acquired through VR training.

7.3.3 Improving Skills Acquisition and Application

VR is particularly effective in improving skills acquisition and application. Traditional training methods often rely on theoretical explanations and demonstrations, which may not fully prepare employees for real-world scenarios. VR, on the other hand, allows employees to practice their skills in realistic and challenging environments, enabling them to develop and refine their abilities.

Through VR simulations, employees can repeatedly practice complex tasks and procedures until they achieve mastery. This repetitive practice enhances muscle memory and procedural knowledge, leading to improved performance and efficiency. Moreover, VR training can simulate high-stress situations, such as emergency response or customer interactions, allowing employees to develop the necessary skills to handle such situations effectively.

7.3.4 Fostering Collaboration and Teamwork

Collaboration and teamwork are essential for the success of any organization. VR training offers unique opportunities to foster collaboration and teamwork among employees. By creating shared virtual environments, employees can collaborate and interact with each other, regardless of their physical locations.

VR enables employees to work together on complex tasks, solve problems collectively, and communicate effectively in a virtual space. This collaborative learning experience promotes teamwork, communication skills, and the ability to work effectively in diverse teams. Employees can learn from each other's perspectives and experiences, leading to a more inclusive and collaborative work culture.

Furthermore, VR training can simulate realistic team-based scenarios, such as crisis management or project coordination, allowing employees to practice and refine their teamwork skills. This hands-on experience in a virtual environment prepares employees to work seamlessly as a team in real-world situations.

In conclusion, VR has a significant impact on employee performance and engagement in corporate training. By enhancing learning outcomes, increasing motivation and retention, improving skills acquisition and application, and fostering collaboration and teamwork, VR transforms the way employees learn and develop their skills. HR managers can leverage the power of VR to create immersive and effective training programs that drive employee performance and engagement to new heights.

Case study

Bank of America

8.1 Overview of Bank of America's VR Training Program

Bank of America, one of the largest financial institutions in the United States, has embraced virtual reality (VR) technology to enhance its corporate training programs. By leveraging the immersive and interactive nature of VR, Bank of America has revolutionized the way it trains its employees, resulting in improved performance, increased engagement, and enhanced learning outcomes.

8.1.1 Background

Bank of America recognized the need to modernize its training methods to keep pace with the rapidly evolving financial industry. Traditional training methods, such as classroom lectures and e-learning modules, were no longer sufficient to meet the demands of a dynamic and complex banking environment. The organization sought a solution that would provide employees with realistic and hands-on experiences, allowing them to develop the necessary skills and knowledge to excel in their roles.

8.1.2 Implementation

Bank of America partnered with VR technology providers to develop a comprehensive VR training program. The program encompasses various aspects of banking, including customer service, sales, compliance, and risk management. Through the use of VR headsets and controllers, employees are immersed in realistic virtual environments that simulate real-life scenarios they may encounter in their day-to-day work.

8.1.3 Training Modules

Bank of America's VR training program consists of a series of modules designed to address specific training needs. Each module focuses on a particular skill or competency and provides employees with opportunities to practice and refine their abilities in a safe and controlled environment. Some of the key training modules include:

8.1.3.1 Customer Service Excellence

This module allows employees to interact with virtual customers and practice delivering exceptional customer service. Through realistic scenarios, employees learn how to handle various customer inquiries, resolve issues, and provide personalized recommendations. The immersive nature of VR enables employees to develop empathy and communication skills, leading to improved customer satisfaction.

8.1.3.2 Sales Techniques

In this module, employees are immersed in virtual sales environments where they can practice their sales techniques. They learn how to identify customer needs, overcome objections, and close deals effectively. The interactive nature of VR allows employees to receive immediate feedback on their performance, enabling them to refine their sales skills and increase their success rates.

8.1.3.3 Compliance and Risk Management

Bank of America places a strong emphasis on compliance and risk management. The VR training program includes modules that educate employees on regulatory requirements, ethical practices, and risk mitigation strategies. Through realistic simulations, employees learn how to identify and address potential compliance issues, ensuring that they adhere to industry regulations and maintain the highest standards of integrity.

8.1.4 Success Factors and Lessons Learned

Bank of America's VR training program has yielded significant benefits for the organization and its employees. Some of the key success factors and lessons learned include:

8.1.4.1 Increased Engagement and Motivation

The immersive and interactive nature of VR training has significantly increased employee engagement and motivation. Employees are more actively involved in the learning process, as they can explore and interact with virtual environments. This heightened engagement translates into improved knowledge retention and application of skills in real-world scenarios.

8.1.4.2 Realistic and Practical Learning Experiences

VR training provides employees with realistic and practical learning experiences that closely resemble their actual work environments. This enables them to develop the necessary skills and confidence to perform their job responsibilities effectively. By practicing in a virtual setting, employees can make mistakes and learn from them without any negative consequences.

8.1.4.3 Cost and Time Savings

Implementing VR training has resulted in cost and time savings for Bank of America. Traditional training methods often require significant resources, such as hiring trainers, booking training venues, and coordinating schedules. With VR, employees can access training modules at their convenience, eliminating the need for extensive logistical arrangements. Additionally, VR training reduces the time required for employees to become proficient in their roles, allowing them to contribute to the organization's success more quickly.

8.1.5 Impact on Employee Performance and Engagement

Bank of America's VR training program has had a profound impact on employee performance and engagement. Employees who have undergone VR training consistently demonstrate higher levels of competency and confidence in their roles. The immersive nature of VR enables employees to develop a deeper understanding of complex concepts and apply them effectively in real-world situations. As a result, employees are better equipped to meet customer needs, drive sales, and mitigate risks, ultimately contributing to the organization's success.

8.1.6 Recommendations for Other Companies

Based on Bank of America's experience, there are several recommendations for other companies looking to implement VR training programs:

Identify Training Needs: Conduct a thorough analysis of training needs and identify areas where VR can provide the most value. Focus on skills and competencies that require hands-on practice and realistic simulations.

Collaborate with VR Technology Providers: **Partner with experienced VR technology providers to develop customized training modules that align with specific organizational goals and objectives.**

Ensure Accessibility: **Make VR training accessible to all employees by providing the necessary hardware and software infrastructure. Consider factors such as scalability, compatibility, and ease of use when selecting VR equipment.**

Measure Effectiveness: **Implement mechanisms to measure the effectiveness of VR training programs. Collect feedback from employees, track performance metrics, and conduct assessments to evaluate the impact of VR on employee performance and engagement.**

Continuously Improve: **Regularly review and update VR training modules to ensure they remain relevant and aligned with evolving business needs. Incorporate feedback from employees and leverage emerging technologies to enhance the training experience.**

By following these recommendations, companies can unlock the full potential of VR in corporate training, just as Bank of America has done. VR training offers a transformative learning experience that empowers employees to excel in their roles, drive organizational success, and stay ahead in an increasingly competitive business landscape.

8.2 Success Factors and Lessons Learned

In this section, we will explore the success factors and lessons learned from the implementation of virtual reality (VR) training programs at Bank of America. By examining their experiences, we can gain valuable insights into the key factors that contribute to the success of VR training initiatives and learn from their lessons.

8.2.1 Commitment from Leadership

One of the critical success factors for Bank of America's VR training program was the strong commitment from leadership. The top management recognized the potential of VR technology in transforming corporate training and actively supported its implementation. This commitment was evident in the allocation of resources, including budget and personnel, to ensure the program's success. By having leadership buy-in, Bank of America was able to overcome any resistance or skepticism from employees and stakeholders, paving the way for a smooth implementation process.

8.2.2 Alignment with Training Objectives

Bank of America's VR training program was designed with a clear alignment to the organization's training objectives. The training content and scenarios were carefully crafted to address specific skill gaps and enhance employee performance in critical areas. By focusing on the specific needs of the organization, Bank of America was able to create a targeted and impactful VR training program that directly contributed to the overall training goals.

8.2.3 Customization and Personalization

Bank of America recognized the importance of customization and personalization in their VR training program. They understood that different employees have varying learning styles and preferences. To cater to these individual needs, Bank of America developed a flexible VR training platform that allowed employees to customize their learning experience. This customization features empowered employees to take ownership of their learning journey, resulting in higher engagement and motivation.

8.2.4 Integration with Existing Training Methods

Bank of America successfully integrated VR training into their existing training methods. They recognized that VR should not replace traditional training approaches but rather complement them. By strategically incorporating VR into their blended learning approach, Bank of America was able to leverage the strengths of both virtual and traditional training methods. This integration ensured a seamless transition for employees and maximized the effectiveness of the overall training program.

8.2.5 Continuous Evaluation and Improvement

Bank of America's VR training program was not a one-time implementation but an ongoing process of evaluation and improvement. They established a feedback loop with employees to gather insights and identify areas for improvement. This continuous evaluation allowed Bank of America to refine their VR training content, scenarios, and delivery methods based on real-time feedback. By constantly iterating and enhancing their VR training program, Bank of America ensured its relevance and effectiveness in meeting the evolving needs of their employees.

8.2.6 Employee Support and Training

Bank of America recognized the importance of providing comprehensive support and training to employees to ensure the successful adoption of VR technology. They conducted extensive training sessions to familiarize employees with the VR hardware and software, as well as the navigation and interaction within the virtual environment. By investing in employee training and support, Bank of America minimized any potential barriers to adoption and ensured a smooth transition to VR training.

8.2.7 Measuring and Demonstrating ROI

Bank of America understood the importance of measuring the return on investment (ROI) of their VR training program. They established key performance indicators (KPIs) to track the impact of VR training on employee performance and engagement. By collecting and analyzing data, Bank of America was able to demonstrate the tangible benefits of VR training, such as improved learning outcomes, increased employee satisfaction, and reduced training costs. This data-driven approach not only justified the investment in VR training but also provided valuable insights for future program enhancements.

8.2.8 Collaboration and Knowledge Sharing

Bank of America fostered a culture of collaboration and knowledge sharing throughout the implementation of their VR training program. They encouraged employees to share their experiences, best practices, and lessons learned, creating a supportive community of VR training enthusiasts. This collaborative approach not only accelerated the learning curve for employees but also facilitated the continuous improvement of the VR training program.

8.2.9 Scalability and Sustainability

Bank of America designed their VR training program with scalability and sustainability in mind. They developed a robust infrastructure that could support the growing demand for VR training across the organization. By investing in scalable hardware and software solutions, Bank of America ensured that their VR training program could accommodate the needs of a large and diverse workforce. Additionally, they established a dedicated team to oversee the program's sustainability, ensuring its long-term success and relevance.

8.2.10 Employee Recognition and Rewards

Bank of America recognized the importance of employee recognition and rewards in driving engagement and motivation. They implemented a system to acknowledge and reward employees who actively participated in the VR training program and demonstrated exceptional performance. This recognition not only incentivized employees to actively engage with the VR training but also created a positive and supportive learning environment.

By considering these success factors and lessons learned from Bank of America's VR training program, HR managers can gain valuable insights into the key elements that contribute to the success of VR training initiatives. By applying these lessons to their own organizations, HR managers can maximize the potential of VR technology in transforming corporate training and driving employee engagement and performance.

8.3 Impact on Employee Performance and Engagement

Virtual reality (VR) has the potential to significantly impact employee performance and engagement in corporate training programs. By providing immersive and interactive learning experiences, VR can enhance employee learning, motivation, and skill acquisition. In this section, we will explore the specific ways in which VR can positively influence employee performance and engagement.

8.3.1 Enhanced Learning Experience

One of the key benefits of VR in corporate training is its ability to create realistic and immersive learning environments. Traditional training methods often rely on lectures, presentations, and written materials, which can be passive and less engaging for employees. In contrast, VR allows employees to actively participate in simulated scenarios, making the learning experience more interactive and memorable.

Through VR, employees can practice real-life tasks and situations in a safe and controlled environment. For example, in a customer service training program, employees can interact with virtual customers and handle various scenarios, such as handling complaints or resolving conflicts. This hands-on experience enables employees to apply their knowledge and skills in a realistic setting, leading to better learning outcomes and improved performance.

8.3.2 Increased Motivation and Retention

Traditional training methods often struggle to maintain employee motivation and engagement.

Employees may feel disengaged or bored during lengthy training sessions, leading to reduced retention of information. VR can address these challenges by providing a more engaging and interactive learning experience.

By immersing employees in virtual environments, VR training programs can capture their attention and maintain their interest throughout the training session. The interactive nature of VR allows employees to actively participate and make decisions, which can increase their motivation to learn and retain information. Studies have shown that VR training can lead to higher knowledge retention rates compared to traditional training methods.

8.3.3 Improved Skills Acquisition and Application

VR offers a unique opportunity for employees to acquire and apply new skills in a realistic and practical manner. Through simulated scenarios, employees can practice and refine their skills in a safe environment before applying them in real-life situations.

For example, in a manufacturing training program, employees can use VR to learn how to operate complex machinery or perform intricate tasks. They can practice these skills repeatedly until they feel confident and proficient. This hands-on approach to learning allows employees to develop their skills more effectively and efficiently, leading to improved performance on the job.

Furthermore, VR training can also help employees transfer their newly acquired skills to real-life situations. By simulating realistic work scenarios, employees can bridge the gap between training and actual job performance. This transfer of skills can lead to increased employee confidence and competence, ultimately enhancing their overall performance and productivity.

8.3.4 Enhanced Collaboration and Teamwork

Collaboration and teamwork are essential for the success of any organization. VR can facilitate and enhance these aspects by providing employees with opportunities to collaborate and work together in virtual environments.

Through VR, employees can engage in team-based activities and simulations, regardless of their physical location. They can collaborate on projects, solve problems, and make decisions as a team, fostering a sense of camaraderie and teamwork. VR can also simulate realistic work scenarios that require collaboration, such as crisis management or group problem-solving exercises.

By promoting collaboration and teamwork, VR training programs can improve employee engagement and performance. Employees who feel connected and supported by their colleagues are more likely to be motivated and productive in their work.

In conclusion, VR has the potential to significantly impact employee performance and engagement in corporate training. By providing immersive and interactive learning experiences, VR can enhance the learning experience, increase motivation and retention, improve skills acquisition and application, and foster collaboration and teamwork. As more organizations recognize the benefits of VR in training, it is crucial for HR managers to consider its potential impact on employee performance and engagement when implementing VR training programs.

Case study

Verizon

9.1 Overview of Verizon's VR Training Program

Verizon, one of the leading telecommunications companies in the world, has embraced the power of virtual reality (VR) in its corporate training programs. By leveraging VR technology, Verizon has revolutionized the way it trains its employees, providing them with immersive and interactive learning experiences. In this section, we will explore the key aspects of Verizon's VR training program, including its objectives, implementation strategies, and the impact it has had on employee performance and engagement.

9.1.1 Objectives of Verizon's VR Training Program

Verizon's VR training program aims to enhance the effectiveness and efficiency of its employee training initiatives. By incorporating VR technology, the company seeks to create a more engaging and realistic learning environment that enables employees to acquire and apply new skills more effectively. The program focuses on various areas, including customer service, technical skills, and leadership development.

9.1.2 Implementation Strategies

To implement its VR training program, Verizon has collaborated with industry-leading VR developers and training experts. The company has invested in state-of-the-art VR hardware and software, ensuring that its employees have access to the latest immersive technologies. Verizon has also established dedicated VR training centers equipped with VR headsets, motion controllers, and other necessary equipment.

The training content is developed in-house by a team of subject matter experts and instructional designers. They work closely with VR developers to create realistic and interactive scenarios that simulate real-world situations. These scenarios allow employees to practice their skills in a safe and controlled environment, providing them with valuable hands-on experience.

Verizon has also integrated its VR training program with its learning management system (LMS), enabling employees to track their progress and access training materials conveniently. The LMS provides a centralized platform for employees to review training modules, complete assessments, and receive feedback from trainers.

9.1.3 Impact on Employee Performance and Engagement

Verizon's VR training program has had a significant impact on employee performance and engagement. By providing employees with immersive and interactive learning experiences, the program has increased their motivation and retention of knowledge. The realistic simulations and hands-on practice enable employees to develop their skills more effectively, leading to improved performance in their roles.

The program has also fostered collaboration and teamwork among employees. Through multiplayer VR experiences, employees can engage in virtual team-building exercises and problem-solving activities. This collaborative approach has not only strengthened relationships among team members but has also enhanced their ability to work together effectively in real-world scenarios.

Furthermore, Verizon's VR training program has resulted in higher levels of employee engagement. The immersive nature of VR creates a sense of presence and excitement, making the learning experience more enjoyable and memorable. Employees are more likely to actively participate in training sessions and apply the knowledge and skills they have acquired in their day-to-day work.

9.1.4 Recommendations for Other Companies

Based on Verizon's success with its VR training program, there are several recommendations for other companies looking to implement VR in their corporate training initiatives:

Identify training needs: Conduct a thorough analysis of your organization's training needs and identify areas where VR can provide the most value. Focus on skills that require hands-on practice or involve high-risk scenarios.

Collaborate with experts: Partner with VR developers and training experts who have experience in creating immersive and effective training content. Their expertise can help ensure the success of your VR training program.

Invest in quality hardware and software: Choose VR hardware and software that meet your organization's specific training requirements. Consider factors such as ease of use, scalability, and compatibility with existing systems.

Integrate with existing training methods: Integrate VR training seamlessly with your existing training methods and platforms. This will allow employees to access training materials and track their progress conveniently.

Measure effectiveness: Implement mechanisms to measure the effectiveness of your VR training program. Collect feedback from employees, track performance metrics, and analyze the impact on employee engagement and performance.

By following these recommendations, companies can leverage the power of VR to transform their corporate training programs, just as Verizon has done successfully.

In the next section, we will explore another case study, focusing on Hilton's VR training program, and the lessons learned from their implementation.

9.2 Success Factors and Lessons Learned

In this section, we will explore the success factors and lessons learned from Verizon's virtual reality (VR) training program. Verizon, a leading telecommunications company, has been at the forefront of leveraging VR technology to enhance their corporate training initiatives. By examining their experiences, we can gain valuable insights into the key factors that contribute to the success of VR training programs and learn from their lessons.

9.2.1 Commitment from Leadership

One of the critical success factors for Verizon's VR training program was the strong commitment from leadership. The company's top executives recognized the potential of VR technology in transforming their training programs and actively supported its implementation. This commitment was evident in the allocation of resources, both financial and human, to ensure the program's success. By having leadership buy-in, Verizon was able to overcome any initial skepticism and resistance to change, paving the way for a successful VR training program.

9.2.2 Alignment with Business Objectives

Verizon's VR training program was designed with a clear alignment with the company's business objectives. The training content was tailored to address specific skill gaps and challenges faced by employees in their day-to-day roles. By focusing on relevant and practical training scenarios, Verizon ensured that the VR training program directly contributed to improving employee performance and productivity. This alignment with business objectives not only increased the effectiveness of the training but also demonstrated the tangible value of VR technology in achieving organizational goals.

9.2.3 Collaboration with Subject Matter Experts

Verizon recognized the importance of involving subject matter experts (SMEs) in the development of their VR training program. SMEs provided valuable insights and expertise in designing realistic and immersive training scenarios that closely mirrored real-world situations. By collaborating with SMEs, Verizon ensured that the training content was accurate, up-to-date, and aligned with industry best practices. This collaboration also helped in gaining the trust and support of employees, as they could see the relevance and applicability of the training to their roles.

9.2.4 User-Centric Design

A key lesson learned from Verizon's VR training program was the importance of user-centric design. The company invested significant time and effort in understanding the needs and preferences of their employees to create a training experience that was engaging and effective. User feedback was actively sought throughout the development process, and iterative improvements were made based on this feedback. By prioritizing the user experience, Verizon ensured that the VR training program was well-received and embraced by employees, leading to higher engagement and knowledge retention.

9.2.5 Integration with Existing Training Methods

Verizon recognized that VR training should not replace existing training methods but rather complement them. The company integrated VR training seamlessly into their broader training ecosystem, leveraging the strengths of each method. For example, VR was used for immersive and hands-on training experiences, while traditional classroom training and e-learning were used for theoretical knowledge transfer. This integration allowed Verizon to maximize the benefits of VR technology while maintaining a holistic and comprehensive approach to training.

9.2.6 Continuous Evaluation and Improvement

Verizon's VR training program was not a one-time implementation but an ongoing initiative that underwent continuous evaluation and improvement. The company regularly collected data and feedback from trainees to assess the effectiveness of the training and identify areas for improvement. This data-driven approach allowed Verizon to make informed decisions about the program's design, content, and delivery methods. By continuously iterating and refining the VR training program, Verizon ensured that it remained relevant, impactful, and aligned with the evolving needs of their employees.

9.2.7 Change Management and Communication

Verizon recognized that introducing VR technology into their training program required effective change management and communication strategies. The company proactively addressed any concerns or resistance to change by providing clear and transparent communication about the benefits and objectives of the VR training program. They also provided comprehensive training and support to employees to ensure a smooth transition to the new training method. By actively managing the change process and fostering a culture of openness and collaboration, Verizon successfully navigated the challenges associated with implementing VR training.

9.2.8 Scalability and Sustainability

Scalability and sustainability were key considerations for Verizon's VR training program. The company ensured that the infrastructure and resources required for VR training were scalable to accommodate the growing needs of their workforce. They also established processes and guidelines for content creation and maintenance to ensure the long-term sustainability of the program. By planning for scalability and sustainability from the outset, Verizon was able to future-proof their

VR training program and maximize its impact over time.

9.2.9 Measuring and Demonstrating ROI

Verizon recognized the importance of measuring and demonstrating the return on investment (ROI) of their VR training program. They established clear metrics and evaluation methods to assess the program's impact on employee performance, engagement, and business outcomes. By collecting and analyzing data, Verizon was able to quantify the tangible benefits of VR training, such as improved productivity, reduced errors, and increased employee satisfaction. This data-driven approach not only justified the investment in VR technology but also provided valuable insights for further program enhancements.

By examining the success factors and lessons learned from Verizon's VR training program, HR managers can gain valuable insights into the key considerations and strategies for implementing VR training in their own organizations. By leveraging these insights, organizations can unlock the full potential of VR technology to transform their corporate training initiatives and drive employee engagement, performance, and productivity.

9.3 Impact on Employee Performance and Engagement

Virtual Reality (VR) has proven to have a significant impact on employee performance and engagement in corporate training programs. By immersing employees in realistic and interactive virtual environments, VR training enhances learning outcomes, increases motivation, and fosters a sense of collaboration and teamwork. In this section, we will explore the specific ways in which VR positively influences employee performance and engagement.

9.3.1 Enhanced Learning Experience

One of the key advantages of VR in corporate training is its ability to provide a highly immersive and realistic learning experience. Traditional training methods often struggle to capture employees' attention and maintain their engagement. However, VR training offers a unique opportunity to create interactive and engaging scenarios that simulate real-life situations.

By placing employees in virtual environments that closely resemble their work environment, VR training allows them to practice and apply their skills in a safe and controlled setting. This hands-on experience enables employees to learn by doing, which has been proven to be a highly effective learning method. As a result, employees are better equipped to transfer their newly acquired knowledge and skills to their actual job tasks, leading to improved performance and productivity.

9.3.2 Increased Motivation and Retention

Traditional training methods often struggle to keep employees motivated and engaged throughout the learning process. However, VR training has been shown to significantly increase motivation and retention rates. The immersive nature of VR creates a sense of excitement and curiosity, making employees more eager to participate in the training.

Moreover, VR training provides immediate feedback and personalized learning experiences, which further enhances motivation. Employees can see the direct impact of their actions within the virtual environment, allowing them to understand the consequences of their decisions and actions. This real-time feedback helps employees to identify areas for improvement and encourages them to actively engage in the learning process.

Additionally, VR training has been found to improve information retention. Studies have shown that the combination of visual, auditory, and kinesthetic learning in VR leads to better memory recall compared to traditional training methods. The ability to interact with virtual objects and scenarios enhances the encoding and retrieval of information, resulting in improved long-term retention.

9.3.3 Improved Skills Acquisition and Application

VR training offers a unique opportunity for employees to acquire and apply new skills in a realistic and immersive environment. By simulating real-life scenarios, employees can practice their skills and receive immediate feedback on their performance. This iterative process allows employees to refine their skills and build confidence in their abilities.

Furthermore, VR training enables employees to experience situations that are difficult to replicate in traditional training settings. For example, employees can practice handling high-stress situations, dealing with difficult customers, or making critical decisions in a safe and controlled environment. This exposure to challenging scenarios helps employees develop the necessary skills and competencies to handle similar situations in their actual job roles.

The ability to apply newly acquired skills in a virtual environment also reduces the risk of errors and mistakes in real-life situations. Employees can make and learn from their mistakes without any negative consequences, leading to improved performance and efficiency in their job tasks.

9.3.4 Fostering Collaboration and Teamwork

Collaboration and teamwork are essential for the success of any organization. VR training provides a unique platform for employees to collaborate and work together in a virtual environment. By simulating team-based scenarios, employees can practice effective communication, problem-solving, and decision-making as a team.

VR training also breaks down geographical barriers, allowing employees from different locations to collaborate and learn together. This fosters a sense of unity and shared purpose among employees, leading to improved teamwork and collaboration in the workplace.

Furthermore, VR training can be used to facilitate virtual meetings and conferences, enabling employees to interact and collaborate in a virtual space. This not only saves time and resources but also promotes inclusivity and diversity by providing equal opportunities for all employees to participate.

In conclusion, VR training has a profound impact on employee performance and engagement in corporate training programs. By providing an enhanced learning experience, increasing motivation and retention, improving skills acquisition and application, and fostering collaboration and teamwork, VR training revolutionizes the way organizations train their employees. As more companies embrace VR technology, the potential for transforming corporate training becomes even greater.

Case study

Hilton

10.1 Overview of Hilton's VR Training Program

Hilton, one of the world's leading hospitality companies, has embraced the power of virtual reality (VR) to revolutionize its corporate training programs. By leveraging immersive technology, Hilton has been able to create a dynamic and engaging learning experience for its employees, resulting in improved performance and increased customer satisfaction.

10.1.1 Embracing VR for Training Excellence

Hilton recognized the potential of VR to transform its training programs and enhance the skills and knowledge of its employees. The company understood that traditional training methods often fell short in providing a realistic and interactive learning environment. With VR, Hilton aimed to bridge this gap and create a training program that would immerse employees in lifelike scenarios, allowing them to practice and refine their skills in a safe and controlled environment.

10.1.2 VR Training Scenarios at Hilton

Hilton's VR training program encompasses a wide range of scenarios that are tailored to the specific needs of its employees. For example, front desk staff undergo training simulations that involve handling various customer service scenarios, such as check-in and check-out processes, handling guest complaints, and managing reservations. By experiencing these scenarios in a virtual setting, employees can develop the necessary skills and confidence to handle real-life situations effectively. Similarly, housekeeping staff undergo VR training that simulates different room setups, cleaning procedures, and safety protocols. This immersive training allows employees to familiarize themselves with the hotel's standards and procedures, ensuring consistent quality and efficiency in their work.

10.1.3 Benefits and Outcomes

Hilton's VR training program has yielded numerous benefits for the company and its employees. Firstly, the immersive nature of VR training has significantly increased employee engagement and motivation. By providing a realistic and interactive learning experience, employees are more likely to be actively involved in the training process, leading to better knowledge retention and application.

Secondly, VR training has proven to be highly effective in improving employee performance. By allowing employees to practice their skills in a virtual environment, they can gain confidence and proficiency before applying those skills in real-life situations. This has resulted in enhanced customer service, increased operational efficiency, and improved overall performance metrics.

Furthermore, Hilton has observed a positive impact on employee satisfaction and retention. The innovative and forward-thinking approach to training has positioned Hilton as an employer that invests in the growth and development of its workforce. This has not only attracted top talent but also fostered a culture of continuous learning and improvement within the organization.

10.1.4 Lessons Learned and Best Practices

Hilton's success with VR training can be attributed to several key factors. Firstly, the company recognized the importance of aligning VR training with its overall business objectives and training needs. By identifying specific areas where VR could add value, Hilton was able to design targeted and impactful training programs.

Secondly, Hilton ensured that its VR training content was of high quality and relevance. The scenarios and simulations were carefully crafted to reflect real-life situations and challenges that employees would encounter in their roles. This attention to detail and authenticity contributed to the effectiveness of the training program.

Additionally, Hilton provided comprehensive support and resources to facilitate the adoption and implementation of VR training. This included investing in the necessary hardware and software, providing training for trainers, and establishing a feedback loop to continuously improve the program based on employee input.

10.1.5 Recommendations for Other Companies

Based on Hilton's experience, there are several recommendations for other companies looking to implement VR training programs:

Conduct a thorough needs assessment: Identify the specific areas where VR can add value and align the training program with the organization's goals and objectives.

Invest in high-quality content: Ensure that the VR training scenarios are realistic, relevant, and engaging to maximize the learning experience.

Provide comprehensive support: Allocate resources for the necessary hardware and software, train trainers to facilitate VR training sessions effectively, and establish mechanisms for feedback and continuous improvement.

Measure and evaluate effectiveness: Implement metrics and evaluation methods to assess the impact of VR training on employee performance and overall business outcomes.

Foster a culture of innovation and learning: Encourage employees to embrace VR training as a valuable tool for their professional development and create a supportive environment that promotes continuous learning.

By following these recommendations, companies can leverage the power of VR to transform their training programs and unlock the full potential of their employees.

In the next section, we will explore another case study, focusing on DHL's VR training program, and the lessons learned from their experience.

10.2 Success Factors and Lessons Learned

In this section, we will explore the success factors and lessons learned from Hilton's virtual reality (VR) training program. Hilton, a global hospitality company, has been at the forefront of leveraging VR technology to enhance their corporate training initiatives. By examining their journey, we can gain valuable insights into the key factors that contribute to the success of VR training programs and learn from their experiences.

10.2.1 Commitment from Leadership

One of the critical success factors for Hilton's VR training program was the unwavering commitment from the company's leadership. From the outset, senior executives recognized the potential of VR technology in transforming their training programs. They provided the necessary resources, support, and guidance to ensure the program's success. This commitment trickled down throughout the organization, creating a culture of innovation and openness to new technologies.

10.2.2 Alignment with Business Objectives

Hilton's VR training program was designed with a clear alignment to the company's business objectives. The training modules were developed to address specific skill gaps and challenges faced by employees in their day-to-day roles. By focusing on the areas that directly impacted the company's performance, Hilton ensured that the VR training program delivered tangible results and added value to the organization.

10.2.3 Customization and Personalization

Hilton recognized the importance of customization and personalization in their VR training program. They understood that one size does not fit all when it comes to training, and different employees have varying learning needs. To address this, Hilton developed a range of VR training modules that catered to different job roles and skill levels. This customization allowed employees to receive training that was relevant to their specific roles, enhancing the effectiveness of the program.

10.2.4 Engaging and Interactive Content

The success of Hilton's VR training program can be attributed to the engaging and interactive content they created. The training modules were designed to be immersive and realistic, providing employees with a hands-on learning experience. By simulating real-world scenarios, employees were able to practice their skills in a safe and controlled environment. This interactive approach not only increased engagement but also improved knowledge retention and skill application.

10.2.5 Continuous Evaluation and Improvement

Hilton understood the importance of continuous evaluation and improvement in their VR training program. They regularly collected feedback from employees and trainers to identify areas for improvement. This feedback loop allowed them to make necessary adjustments to the training modules, ensuring that they remained relevant and effective. By embracing a culture of continuous improvement, Hilton was able to enhance the impact of their VR training program over time.

10.2.6 Integration with Existing Training Methods

Another key success factor for Hilton was the seamless integration of VR training with their existing training methods. They recognized that VR was not meant to replace traditional training but rather complement it. Hilton integrated VR modules into their broader training curriculum, combining the benefits of both virtual and in-person training. This integration ensured a holistic and comprehensive learning experience for employees.

10.2.7 Support and Resources for Employees

Hilton understood that the successful implementation of VR training required adequate support and resources for employees. They provided comprehensive training and support to ensure that employees were comfortable using the VR technology. Additionally, Hilton established a dedicated support team to address any technical issues or concerns that employees may have encountered during the training process. This support system played a crucial role in facilitating the adoption and acceptance of VR training among employees.

10.2.8 Measuring and Demonstrating ROI

Hilton recognized the importance of measuring and demonstrating the return on investment (ROI) of their VR training program. They implemented robust evaluation methods to assess the impact of the training on employee performance and engagement. By collecting data and analyzing the results, Hilton was able to quantify the benefits of VR training in terms of improved employee productivity, reduced training costs, and enhanced customer satisfaction. This data-driven approach helped them secure continued support and investment in their VR training program.

10.2.9 Collaboration and Knowledge Sharing

Hilton actively fostered collaboration and knowledge sharing among employees participating in the VR training program. They encouraged employees to share their experiences, insights, and best practices with their colleagues. This collaborative approach not only enhanced the learning experience but also created a sense of community and camaraderie among employees. By leveraging the collective knowledge and expertise of their workforce, Hilton was able to maximize the impact of their VR training program.

10.2.10 Scalability and Sustainability

Lastly, Hilton ensured that their VR training program was scalable and sustainable. They developed a robust infrastructure and framework that could accommodate the growing demand for VR training across their global workforce. Hilton also invested in the continuous development and maintenance of the VR training modules to ensure their relevance and effectiveness over time. This focus on scalability and sustainability allowed Hilton to reap the long-term benefits of their VR training program.

By examining the success factors and lessons learned from Hilton's VR training program, we can gain valuable insights into the key considerations for implementing VR in corporate training. These insights can guide HR managers in designing and implementing their own VR training programs, enabling them to unlock the full potential of immersive learning in their organizations.

10.3 Impact on Employee Performance and Engagement

Virtual reality (VR) has revolutionized corporate training by providing immersive and interactive learning experiences. In this section, we will explore the impact of VR on employee performance and engagement. We will examine how VR training programs have enhanced employee skills, increased motivation, and fostered a culture of continuous learning.

10.3.1 Enhancing Skills Acquisition and Application

One of the key benefits of VR in corporate training is its ability to enhance skills acquisition and application. Traditional training methods often rely on theoretical knowledge and passive learning, which may not effectively translate into practical skills. VR, on the other hand, offers a hands-on approach that allows employees to practice and apply their skills in a realistic and immersive environment.

By simulating real-world scenarios, VR training enables employees to develop and refine their skills in a safe and controlled setting. For example, in the hospitality industry, VR can simulate customer interactions, allowing employees to practice their customer service skills and handle challenging situations. This hands-on experience not only improves their skills but also boosts their confidence in dealing with real-life scenarios.

Furthermore, VR training can provide immediate feedback and performance evaluations, allowing employees to identify areas for improvement and make adjustments in real-time. This personalized feedback helps employees to refine their skills and achieve higher levels of proficiency. As a result, employees are better equipped to perform their job responsibilities effectively, leading to improved overall performance.

10.3.2 Increasing Motivation and Engagement

Traditional training methods often struggle to maintain employee motivation and engagement. Employees may feel disengaged during lengthy lectures or monotonous e-learning modules. VR training, on the other hand, offers a highly engaging and interactive learning experience that captivates employees' attention and keeps them motivated throughout the training process.

The immersive nature of VR creates a sense of presence, making employees feel as if they are physically present in the training environment. This heightened sense of realism and interactivity stimulates employees' curiosity and interest, leading to increased engagement and active participation.

Moreover, VR training allows employees to explore and experiment in a risk-free environment. They can make mistakes, learn from them, and iterate until they achieve the desired outcome. This freedom to learn through trial and error fosters a culture of continuous learning and innovation, as employees are encouraged to think creatively and explore different approaches.

Additionally, VR training can be gamified, incorporating elements of competition, rewards, and challenges. By introducing game-like elements, such as leaderboards, achievements, and virtual rewards, employees are motivated to strive for excellence and improve their performance. This gamification aspect not only enhances engagement but also creates a sense of enjoyment and satisfaction in the learning process.

10.3.3 Improving Employee Performance and Productivity

The impact of VR on employee performance and productivity is significant. By providing realistic and immersive training experiences, VR enables employees to acquire and apply skills more effectively, leading to improved job performance. Employees who undergo VR training are better prepared to handle complex tasks, make informed decisions, and adapt to changing work environments.

Furthermore, VR training can significantly reduce the time required for employee onboarding and skill development. Traditional training methods often involve lengthy classroom sessions and on-the-job training, which can be time-consuming and costly. VR training allows employees to learn at their own pace and provides a standardized and consistent learning experience. This streamlined training process not only saves time but also ensures that all employees receive the same level of training and knowledge.

Moreover, VR training can have a positive impact on employee retention. Employees who receive immersive and engaging training experiences are more likely to feel valued and invested in their organization. They are also more likely to develop a sense of loyalty and commitment, leading to increased employee retention rates.

10.3.4 Fostering Collaboration and Teamwork

In addition to enhancing individual performance, VR training can also foster collaboration and teamwork among employees. VR simulations can recreate collaborative work environments, allowing employees to interact and collaborate with virtual colleagues in real-time.

By working together in a virtual environment, employees can practice and improve their communication, problem-solving, and teamwork skills. They can learn to collaborate effectively, delegate tasks, and resolve conflicts, all within a safe and controlled setting. This collaborative learning experience not only strengthens individual skills but also promotes a sense of camaraderie and teamwork among employees.

Furthermore, VR training can facilitate cross-functional collaboration by bringing together employees from different departments or locations. Virtual meetings and collaborative projects enable employees to work together regardless of geographical barriers, fostering a culture of inclusivity and diversity.

In conclusion, VR training has a profound impact on employee performance and engagement. By enhancing skills acquisition, increasing motivation, improving performance, and fostering collaboration, VR training programs have the potential to transform corporate training and drive organizational success. As more companies embrace VR technology, it is crucial for HR managers to understand the benefits and leverage its potential to create a highly skilled and engaged workforce.

Case study

DHL

11.1 Overview of DHL's VR Training Program

DHL, one of the world's leading logistics companies, has embraced the power of virtual reality (VR) to revolutionize its corporate training programs. By leveraging immersive technology, DHL has been able to enhance employee learning, improve performance, and drive engagement. In this case study, we will explore the key elements of DHL's VR training program, the success factors that have contributed to its effectiveness, and the lessons learned along the way.

11.1.1 The Need for VR Training at DHL

As a global logistics company, DHL operates in a fast-paced and complex environment. The training needs of its employees are diverse, ranging from warehouse operations to supply chain management. Traditional training methods, such as classroom sessions and e-learning modules, were not fully meeting the requirements of DHL's dynamic workforce. The company recognized the need for a more immersive and interactive training approach that could simulate real-world scenarios and provide hands-on experience.

11.1.2 Designing the VR Training Program

DHL collaborated with VR experts and instructional designers to develop a comprehensive VR training program. The first step was to identify the specific training areas where VR could make the most impact. These included warehouse operations, forklift training, and hazardous materials handling. By focusing on these critical areas, DHL aimed to improve employee safety, efficiency, and overall performance.

The VR training content was carefully crafted to replicate real-world scenarios that employees would encounter in their day-to-day work. For example, warehouse operators could practice navigating through a virtual warehouse, picking and packing items, and operating forklifts in a safe and controlled environment. The training scenarios were designed to be highly realistic, providing employees with a sense of presence and immersion.

11.1.3 Implementation and Deployment

To ensure the successful implementation of the VR training program, DHL invested in the necessary hardware and software infrastructure. This included high-quality VR headsets, motion controllers, and powerful computers capable of running the VR simulations smoothly. DHL also established dedicated VR training centers at select locations, equipped with the necessary VR equipment and facilities.

The deployment of the VR training program was carefully planned to ensure maximum accessibility and participation. DHL provided comprehensive training to its employees on how to use the VR equipment and navigate the virtual environments.

The program was made available to employees across different locations, allowing for consistent and standardized training experiences.

11.1.4 Success Factors and Lessons Learned

DHL's VR training program has yielded significant success and positive outcomes. The immersive nature of the training has resulted in higher engagement levels among employees, leading to improved knowledge retention and skill acquisition. The ability to practice in realistic scenarios has also boosted employee confidence and competence in their job roles.

One of the key success factors of DHL's VR training program is the integration of feedback loops. Employees are encouraged to provide feedback on their training experiences, allowing DHL to continuously improve and refine the VR simulations. This iterative approach has helped to address any potential issues or limitations of the VR training program, ensuring its ongoing effectiveness.

DHL has also learned valuable lessons throughout the implementation of its VR training program. It is crucial to have a clear understanding of the training objectives and align them with the capabilities of VR technology. Additionally, ongoing support and training for employees are essential to ensure their comfort and proficiency in using the VR equipment and software.

11.1.5 Impact on Employee Performance and Engagement

The impact of DHL's VR training program on employee performance and engagement has been remarkable. Employees who have undergone VR training have demonstrated increased efficiency and accuracy in their job tasks. The ability to practice in a realistic and immersive environment has translated into improved on-the-job performance, leading to higher customer satisfaction and operational excellence.

Moreover, the VR training program has significantly enhanced employee engagement and motivation. The interactive and experiential nature of VR has made the training more enjoyable and memorable for employees. This has resulted in a higher level of enthusiasm and commitment to continuous learning and development.

11.1.6 Recommendations for Other Companies

Based on the success of DHL's VR training program, there are several recommendations for other companies looking to implement VR in their corporate training:

Identify the specific training areas where VR can have the most impact and align them with the organization's strategic objectives.

Collaborate with VR experts and instructional designers to develop engaging and realistic training content.

Invest in the necessary hardware and software infrastructure to support the VR training program. Provide comprehensive training and support to employees to ensure their comfort and proficiency in using VR technology.

Establish feedback loops to continuously improve and refine the VR training program based on employee input.

Monitor and measure the impact of the VR training program on employee performance and engagement to demonstrate its effectiveness.

By following these recommendations, companies can unlock the full potential of VR in corporate training and drive meaningful improvements in employee learning, performance, and engagement.

11.2 Success Factors and Lessons Learned

In this section, we will explore the success factors and lessons learned from DHL's implementation of virtual reality (VR) in their corporate training program. DHL, a global logistics company, recognized the potential of VR technology to enhance their training initiatives and improve employee performance and engagement. By examining their experience, we can gain valuable insights into the key factors that contributed to their success and the lessons learned along the way.

11.2.1 Commitment from Leadership

One of the critical success factors for DHL's VR training program was the commitment and support from top-level leadership. The company's executives recognized the value of immersive learning and were willing to invest in the necessary resources to implement VR technology effectively. This commitment provided the program with the necessary funding, infrastructure, and organizational support, ensuring its success.

11.2.2 Alignment with Training Objectives

DHL's VR training program was designed with a clear alignment to the company's training objectives. By identifying specific areas where VR could provide the most significant impact, DHL was able to develop targeted training modules that addressed their employees' needs. This alignment ensured that the VR training program was relevant, practical, and directly contributed to the improvement of employee performance.

11.2.3 Collaboration with Subject Matter Experts

DHL recognized the importance of collaborating with subject matter experts (SMEs) throughout the development and implementation of their VR training program. By involving SMEs from various departments, DHL ensured that the training content was accurate, up-to-date, and aligned with industry best practices. This collaboration also helped to identify specific training scenarios and challenges that could be effectively addressed through VR technology.

11.2.4 User-Centric Design

A user-centric design approach was a crucial factor in the success of DHL's VR training program. The company focused on creating an immersive and engaging learning experience that catered to the needs and preferences of their employees. By considering the user's perspective, DHL was able to design training scenarios that were realistic, interactive, and provided a high level of engagement. This user-centric approach contributed to increased motivation, retention, and skills acquisition among the employees.

11.2.5 Continuous Evaluation and Improvement

DHL understood the importance of continuous evaluation and improvement in their VR training program. They implemented a robust feedback mechanism that allowed employees to provide input on the effectiveness of the training modules. This feedback was used to identify areas for improvement and make necessary adjustments to enhance the overall training experience. By continuously evaluating and refining the program, DHL ensured that it remained relevant and effective in meeting their training objectives.

11.2.6 Integration with Existing Training Methods

DHL successfully integrated VR technology with their existing training methods, leveraging the strengths of both traditional and immersive learning approaches. They recognized that VR was not meant to replace all training methods but rather complement them. By strategically integrating VR into their training curriculum, DHL was able to provide a blended learning experience that combined the benefits of hands-on practice in a virtual environment with classroom instruction and on-the-job training.

11.2.7 Scalability and Accessibility

DHL's VR training program was designed with scalability and accessibility in mind. The company ensured that the program could be easily scaled to accommodate a large number of employees across different locations. They also made efforts to ensure that the VR training content was accessible to employees with varying levels of technical expertise. By addressing these scalability and accessibility challenges, DHL was able to maximize the reach and impact of their VR training program.

11.2.8 Continuous Support and Training

DHL recognized that the successful implementation of VR training required ongoing support and training for both employees and trainers. They provided comprehensive training programs to familiarize employees with the VR technology and ensure they were comfortable using it. Additionally, DHL offered continuous support to address any technical issues or challenges that arose during the training process. This commitment to support and training contributed to the overall success and adoption of the VR training program.

11.2.9 Measuring and Demonstrating ROI

DHL understood the importance of measuring and demonstrating the return on investment (ROI) of their VR training program. They implemented robust evaluation methods to assess the impact of the training on employee performance and engagement. By collecting data and analyzing the results, DHL was able to demonstrate the tangible benefits of the VR training program, such as improved productivity, reduced errors, and increased employee satisfaction. This data-driven approach helped to secure ongoing support and investment in the VR training program.

11.2.10 Lessons Learned

Throughout their journey of implementing VR in their corporate training program, DHL learned several valuable lessons. They realized the importance of conducting thorough research and analysis before implementing VR, ensuring that it aligns with the organization's goals and objectives. DHL also emphasized the need for effective change management strategies to address any resistance or skepticism from employees. Additionally, they highlighted the significance of ongoing evaluation and improvement to ensure the program's long-term success.

By understanding these success factors and lessons learned from DHL's experience, HR managers can gain valuable insights into implementing VR in their own corporate training programs. By leveraging these insights, organizations can unlock the full potential of immersive learning and revolutionize their training initiatives.

11.3 Impact on Employee Performance and Engagement

Virtual Reality (VR) has proven to have a significant impact on employee performance and engagement in corporate training programs. By immersing employees in realistic and interactive virtual environments, VR training enhances learning outcomes, increases motivation and retention, improves skills acquisition and application, and fosters collaboration and teamwork. In this section, we will explore the specific ways in which VR positively influences employee performance and engagement.

11.3.1 Enhanced Learning Experience

One of the key advantages of VR in corporate training is its ability to provide a highly immersive and engaging learning experience. Traditional training methods often struggle to capture employees' attention and maintain their interest. However, VR training offers a unique opportunity to create realistic and interactive scenarios that simulate real-world situations. By placing employees in these virtual environments, they can actively participate in the learning process, making it more memorable and impactful.

The immersive nature of VR allows employees to experience training scenarios firsthand, enabling them to develop a deeper understanding of the subject matter. For example, in a customer service training program, employees can interact with virtual customers and practice their skills in a safe and controlled environment. This hands-on experience enhances their learning and enables them to apply their knowledge more effectively in real-life situations.

11.3.2 Increased Motivation and Retention

Traditional training methods often struggle to maintain employees' motivation and interest throughout the learning process. However, VR training has been shown to significantly increase motivation and retention rates. The immersive and interactive nature of VR creates a sense of excitement and engagement that traditional methods cannot replicate.

When employees are actively engaged in the learning process, they are more likely to retain the information and skills they acquire. VR training provides a multisensory experience, incorporating visual, auditory, and kinesthetic elements, which enhances information processing and memory retention. As a result, employees are better equipped to apply their newly acquired knowledge and skills in their day-to-day work.

11.3.3 Improved Skills Acquisition and Application

VR training offers a unique opportunity for employees to practice and refine their skills in a realistic and risk-free environment. By simulating real-world scenarios, employees can develop and hone their skills without the fear of making mistakes or causing harm. This hands-on approach to training allows employees to learn from their experiences and receive immediate feedback, enabling them to improve their performance more effectively.

For example, in a manufacturing setting, employees can use VR simulations to practice operating complex machinery or performing intricate tasks. By repeatedly practicing these skills in a virtual environment, employees can build muscle memory and develop a high level of proficiency. This translates into improved performance and productivity in their actual work settings.

11.3.4 Fostering Collaboration and Teamwork

VR training can also have a positive impact on collaboration and teamwork within organizations. By creating shared virtual environments, employees can collaborate and interact with each other, regardless of their physical locations. This is particularly beneficial for organizations with geographically dispersed teams or remote workers. Through VR training, employees can engage in collaborative activities such as problem-solving, decision-making, and role-playing exercises. By working together in a virtual space, employees can develop effective communication and teamwork skills, which are essential for success in today's interconnected and globalized business environment.

Furthermore, VR training can also facilitate cross-functional collaboration by bringing together employees from different departments or teams. This promotes a sense of unity and shared purpose, leading to improved employee engagement and overall organizational performance.

In conclusion, VR training has a profound impact on employee performance and engagement in corporate settings. By providing an immersive and interactive learning experience, VR enhances learning outcomes, increases motivation and retention, improves skills acquisition and application, and fosters collaboration and teamwork. As more organizations recognize the potential of VR in corporate training, it is crucial for HR managers to embrace this technology and leverage its benefits to drive organizational success.

Case study

Presbyterian New York Hospital

12.1 Overview of Presbyterian New York Hospital's VR Training Program

Presbyterian New York Hospital (PNYH) is a renowned healthcare institution that has embraced the power of virtual reality (VR) in its corporate training programs. By leveraging VR technology, PNYH has revolutionized the way it trains its employees, enhancing their skills and knowledge in a highly immersive and engaging manner.

12.1.1 Introduction to PNYH's VR Training Program

PNYH's VR training program is designed to address the unique challenges faced by healthcare professionals in a dynamic and fast-paced environment. The program focuses on various aspects of healthcare, including patient care, surgical procedures, emergency response, and medical equipment operation.

The VR training program at PNYH utilizes cutting-edge VR hardware and software to create realistic and interactive simulations. These simulations replicate real-life scenarios, allowing employees to practice their skills and decision-making abilities in a safe and controlled environment.

12.1.2 Key Features and Components of PNYH's VR Training Program

PNYH's VR training program incorporates several key features and components that contribute to its effectiveness and success:

1. Realistic Simulations

The VR simulations developed by PNYH accurately replicate the hospital environment, including patient rooms, operating theaters, emergency rooms, and diagnostic laboratories. These realistic simulations enable employees to experience and navigate through various scenarios, enhancing their familiarity with the hospital setting.

2. Interactive Learning Experiences

PNYH's VR training program promotes active learning through interactive experiences. Employees can engage with virtual patients, medical equipment, and other healthcare professionals, fostering a sense of presence and immersion. This interactivity allows employees to practice their communication, decision-making, and critical thinking skills in a realistic context.

3. Customized Training Modules

PNYH's VR training program offers a range of customized training modules tailored to different roles and departments within the hospital. Whether it's training for nurses, surgeons, or emergency response teams, the program provides targeted and specialized training experiences that address the specific needs of each role.

4. Performance Assessment and Feedback

PNYH's VR training program includes built-in assessment tools that track employees' performance during the simulations. These assessments measure various metrics, such as response time, accuracy, and adherence to protocols. Employees receive immediate feedback on their performance, allowing them to identify areas for improvement and refine their skills.

12.1.3 Success Factors and Lessons Learned

PNYH's VR training program has yielded significant success and positive outcomes for the organization. Several key factors have contributed to its effectiveness:

1. Engagement and Motivation

The immersive nature of VR training at PNYH has significantly increased employee engagement and motivation. The realistic simulations and interactive experiences capture employees' attention and create a sense of excitement, making the learning process more enjoyable and memorable.

2. Skill Transfer and Retention

PNYH has observed a higher level of skill transfer and retention among employees who undergo VR training. The hands-on practice and realistic scenarios enable employees to develop muscle memory and reinforce their knowledge, leading to improved performance in real-life situations.

3. Risk-Free Learning Environment

One of the key advantages of VR training at PNYH is the ability to provide a risk-free learning environment. Employees can make mistakes, learn from them, and refine their skills without any potential harm to patients or equipment. This fosters a culture of continuous learning and experimentation.

4. Collaboration and Teamwork

PNYH's VR training program promotes collaboration and teamwork among healthcare professionals. Employees can participate in multi-player simulations, where they work together to solve complex medical cases or perform surgical procedures. This collaborative approach enhances communication, coordination, and teamwork skills.

12.1.4 Impact on Employee Performance and Engagement

The implementation of VR training at PNYH has had a profound impact on employee performance and engagement:

1. Improved Clinical Skills

Employees who have undergone VR training at PNYH have demonstrated enhanced clinical skills, including diagnostic accuracy, procedural proficiency, and patient care. The hands-on practice and realistic scenarios enable employees to develop and refine their skills in a controlled and immersive environment.

2. Increased Confidence

VR training has boosted employees' confidence in their abilities to handle challenging situations. The realistic simulations and repeated practice instill a sense of competence and self-assurance, empowering employees to make critical decisions with confidence.

3. Enhanced Patient Safety

By providing a risk-free learning environment, VR training at PNYH has contributed to improved patient safety. Employees who have undergone VR training are better equipped to handle emergencies, follow protocols, and make informed decisions, ultimately leading to better patient outcomes.

4. Higher Employee Satisfaction

The implementation of VR training has resulted in higher employee satisfaction at PNYH. Employees appreciate the innovative and engaging approach to learning, which enhances their professional development and job satisfaction. This, in turn, contributes to higher employee retention rates.

12.1.5 Recommendations for Other Companies

Based on the success of PNYH's VR training program, here are some recommendations for other companies looking to implement VR in their corporate training:

Conduct a thorough needs assessment to identify the specific training requirements and objectives.

Invest in high-quality VR hardware and software to ensure a realistic and immersive training experience.

Customize the VR training program to align with the unique needs and roles within the organization.

Provide ongoing support and resources to employees during the VR training process.

Continuously evaluate and measure the effectiveness of the VR training program through performance assessments and feedback.

By following these recommendations, companies can unlock the potential of VR in corporate training and reap the benefits of enhanced employee performance and engagement.

12.2 Recommendations for Other Companies

As you have seen from the case studies of Johnson & Johnson, Chevron, Bank of America, Verizon, Hilton, DHL, and Presbyterian New York Hospital, virtual reality (VR) has the potential to revolutionize corporate training. These companies have successfully implemented VR training programs and have experienced significant benefits in terms of employee performance and engagement. If you are considering introducing VR into your own organization's training initiatives, here are some recommendations to help you get started:

12.2.1 Assess Your Training Needs and Objectives

Before implementing VR training, it is crucial to assess your organization's specific training needs and objectives. Identify the areas where VR can add the most value and address any skill gaps or performance challenges. Conduct a thorough analysis of your current training methods and determine how VR can enhance the learning experience and improve employee engagement. By understanding your training needs and objectives, you can design a VR training program that aligns with your organization's goals.

12.2.2 Start with a Pilot Program

Implementing VR training on a large scale can be a significant investment. To mitigate risks and ensure a successful rollout, consider starting with a pilot program. Select a specific department or a group of employees to participate in the pilot program and gather feedback on the effectiveness of VR training. This will allow you to make any necessary adjustments before scaling up the program across the organization.

12.2.3 Collaborate with VR Experts

To ensure the success of your VR training program, it is essential to collaborate with VR experts. Seek out professionals who have experience in developing VR training content and can provide guidance on the selection of hardware and software. These experts can help you navigate the complexities of VR technology and ensure that your training program is designed to maximize engagement and learning outcomes.

12.2.4 Customize VR Training Content

One of the key advantages of VR training is the ability to create immersive and interactive experiences. Take advantage of this by customizing the VR training content to align with your organization's specific needs. Tailor the scenarios and simulations to reflect real-life situations that employees may encounter in their roles. By customizing the content, you can create a more relevant and engaging training experience for your employees.

12.2.5 Integrate VR with Existing Training Methods

VR training should not replace all existing training methods but rather complement them. Integrate VR into your existing training programs to create a blended learning approach. Combine traditional classroom training, e-learning modules, and VR simulations to provide a comprehensive and well-rounded training experience. This integration will allow employees to benefit from the strengths of each training method and ensure a seamless transition to VR training.

12.2.6 Measure the Effectiveness of VR Training

To evaluate the impact of your VR training program, it is crucial to measure its effectiveness. Define key performance indicators (KPIs) that align with your training objectives and track them throughout the program. Collect data on employee performance, engagement levels, and knowledge retention to assess the success of the VR training. Use this data to make informed decisions about the future of your training initiatives and identify areas for improvement.

12.2.7 Provide Ongoing Support and Training

Implementing VR training requires ongoing support and training for both employees and trainers. Ensure that employees have access to technical support and resources to troubleshoot any issues they may encounter during the training. Additionally, provide training for trainers to familiarize them with the VR technology and equip them with the skills to facilitate VR training sessions effectively. Ongoing support and training will contribute to the long-term success and sustainability of your VR training program.

12.2.8 Foster a Culture of Innovation and Learning

Introducing VR training into your organization requires a culture that embraces innovation and continuous learning. Encourage employees to explore and experiment with the VR technology, fostering a sense of curiosity and creativity. Create opportunities for employees to share their experiences and insights from the VR training, promoting a culture of knowledge sharing and collaboration. By fostering a culture of innovation and learning, you can maximize the benefits of VR training and drive organizational growth.

12.2.9 Stay Updated on Emerging Technologies

VR technology is continuously evolving, and new advancements are being made regularly. Stay updated on emerging technologies and innovations in the VR space to ensure that your training program remains relevant and effective. Attend industry conferences, join professional networks, and engage with VR experts to stay informed about the latest trends and developments. By staying ahead of the curve, you can position your organization as a leader in VR training and leverage the full potential of this transformative technology. Implementing VR training in your organization can be a game-changer for employee engagement and performance. By following these recommendations and learning from the experiences of companies like Johnson & Johnson, Chevron, Bank of America, Verizon, Hilton, DHL, and Presbyterian New York Hospital, you can successfully introduce VR into your corporate training initiatives and unlock the full potential of immersive learning.

Addressing Concerns and Overcoming Resistance

13.1 Common Concerns about VR in Corporate Training

As with any new technology, the introduction of virtual reality (VR) in corporate training comes with its fair share of concerns and apprehensions. While the benefits of VR in enhancing employee engagement and improving training outcomes are well-documented, it is important to address these concerns to ensure a smooth and successful implementation. In this section, we will explore some of the common concerns about VR in corporate training and discuss strategies for addressing them.

13.1.1 Cost and Return on Investment

One of the primary concerns that organizations may have when considering VR for corporate training is the cost involved. VR hardware and software can be expensive, and there may also be additional costs associated with content development and maintenance. However, it is important to consider the long-term benefits and return on investment (ROI) that VR can offer.

Studies have shown that VR training can lead to improved learning outcomes, increased retention rates, and enhanced employee performance. By providing a realistic and immersive learning experience, VR can help employees develop skills more effectively and efficiently. This can result in cost savings in the long run, as employees are better equipped to perform their jobs and make fewer mistakes.

To address concerns about cost, organizations can start by conducting a thorough cost-benefit analysis. This analysis should take into account factors such as the cost of traditional training methods, the potential savings from improved performance, and the scalability of VR training programs. By demonstrating the potential ROI of VR training, organizations can make a strong case for its implementation.

13.1.2 Technical Challenges and Infrastructure Requirements

Another concern that organizations may have is the technical complexity of implementing VR training programs. VR requires specialized hardware and software, and organizations may need to invest in infrastructure upgrades to support the technology. Additionally, there may be concerns about the compatibility of VR systems with existing IT infrastructure.

To address these concerns, organizations should work closely with their IT departments and VR vendors to ensure a smooth implementation. It is important to conduct a thorough assessment of the organization's technical capabilities and requirements before investing in VR technology. This assessment should include considerations such as network bandwidth, hardware compatibility, and software integration.

Furthermore, organizations can consider partnering with VR vendors who offer comprehensive support and training services. These vendors can assist with the setup and maintenance of VR systems, as well as provide technical support and troubleshooting. By leveraging the expertise of VR vendors, organizations can overcome technical challenges and ensure a seamless integration of VR into their training programs.

13.1.3 User Acceptance and Comfort

User acceptance and comfort are valid concerns when introducing VR into corporate training. Some employees may be unfamiliar with VR technology or may have reservations about using it. Additionally, there may be concerns about motion sickness or discomfort associated with wearing VR headsets for extended periods.

To address these concerns, organizations can take a phased approach to VR implementation. This involves gradually introducing VR training programs and providing ample training and support to employees. By offering hands-on demonstrations and workshops, organizations can familiarize employees with VR technology and address any concerns or misconceptions they may have.

It is also important to ensure that VR training experiences are comfortable and user-friendly. This can be achieved by selecting VR hardware that is lightweight and ergonomic, and by providing regular breaks during training sessions to minimize discomfort. Organizations should also consider conducting user satisfaction surveys and gathering feedback from employees to continuously improve the VR training experience.

13.1.4 Data Privacy and Security

Data privacy and security are critical concerns in any training program, and VR is no exception. Organizations must ensure that sensitive employee data is protected and that VR training platforms comply with relevant data protection regulations.

To address these concerns, organizations should carefully evaluate the data privacy and security measures implemented by VR vendors. This includes assessing the encryption protocols used, the storage and transmission of data, and the vendor's compliance with industry standards and regulations.

Additionally, organizations should establish clear policies and guidelines regarding data privacy and security in VR training programs. This includes educating employees about their rights and responsibilities when using VR technology and implementing appropriate access controls and authentication mechanisms.

By addressing concerns about data privacy and security, organizations can build trust and confidence in their VR training programs and ensure the protection of sensitive employee information.

Conclusion

While concerns about VR in corporate training are valid, they can be effectively addressed through careful planning, communication, and collaboration with stakeholders. By addressing concerns related to cost, technical challenges, user acceptance, and data privacy, organizations can pave the way for a successful implementation of VR in their training programs. In the next section, we will discuss strategies for overcoming resistance to

VR adoption and communicating the value of VR training.

13.2 Strategies for Addressing Concerns

As with any new technology, the introduction of virtual reality (VR) in corporate training may raise concerns and resistance among employees and stakeholders. It is important for HR managers to address these concerns and overcome resistance in order to successfully implement VR training programs. In this section, we will discuss some strategies for addressing concerns and ensuring a smooth transition to VR training.

13.2.1 Educate and Inform

One of the most effective strategies for addressing concerns about VR in corporate training is to educate and inform employees and stakeholders about the technology and its benefits. Many concerns arise from a lack of understanding or misconceptions about VR. HR managers should provide clear and concise information about how VR works, its potential applications in training, and the specific benefits it can bring to the organization. By organizing informational sessions, workshops, or webinars, HR managers can provide employees with an opportunity to learn about VR firsthand. They can showcase examples of successful VR training programs in other organizations and explain how VR can enhance the learning experience, improve skills acquisition, and foster collaboration and teamwork. By addressing concerns through education, HR managers can help employees see the value and potential of VR in corporate training.

13.2.2 Addressing Safety Concerns

One common concern about VR in corporate training is the potential for physical discomfort or motion sickness. HR managers should address these concerns by ensuring that the VR hardware and software used in training programs are of high quality and designed to minimize discomfort. They should also provide clear instructions on how to use the VR equipment properly and safely.

Additionally, HR managers can consider implementing a gradual introduction to VR training. This can involve starting with shorter VR sessions and gradually increasing the duration as employees become more comfortable with the technology. By addressing safety concerns and taking steps to minimize discomfort, HR managers can alleviate fears and encourage employees to embrace VR training.

13.2.3 Provide Training and Support

Another effective strategy for addressing concerns about VR in corporate training is to provide comprehensive training and ongoing support to employees. HR managers should ensure that employees receive proper training on how to use the VR equipment and software, as well as guidance on how to navigate the VR training programs.

By offering training sessions or workshops specifically focused on VR training, HR managers can help employees become familiar with the technology and build confidence in using it. They should also establish a support system where employees can seek assistance or ask questions related to VR training. This can include providing access to technical support or assigning dedicated

VR training mentors who can provide guidance and support throughout the learning process.

13.2.4 Addressing Privacy and Data Security Concerns

Privacy and data security are important considerations when implementing VR training programs. HR managers should address concerns about data collection, storage, and usage by implementing robust privacy and security measures. This can include ensuring that VR training platforms comply with relevant data protection regulations and implementing encryption and access controls to safeguard sensitive information.

HR managers should also communicate transparently with employees about the data that will be collected during VR training and how it will be used. By providing clear information about data privacy and security measures, HR managers can alleviate concerns and build trust among employees.

13.2.5 Involve Employees in the Process

To overcome resistance to VR adoption, it is important to involve employees in the decision-making process and seek their input and feedback. HR managers should create opportunities for employees to share their concerns, suggestions, and ideas regarding the implementation of VR training programs.

By involving employees in the process, HR managers can address concerns more effectively and ensure that the VR training programs meet the specific needs and preferences of the workforce. This can also help build a sense of ownership and engagement among employees, making them more receptive to the introduction of VR in corporate training.

13.2.6 Communicate the Benefits

Lastly, HR managers should effectively communicate the benefits of VR training to employees and stakeholders. By highlighting the advantages of VR, such as its ability to create immersive and realistic learning experiences, improve skills acquisition, and enhance employee engagement, HR managers can generate enthusiasm and support for VR training programs. Communicating the benefits can be done through various channels, such as company-wide emails, newsletters, intranet articles, or dedicated VR training information sessions. HR managers should emphasize how VR training can contribute to individual and organizational growth, career development, and overall performance improvement. By effectively communicating the value of VR training, HR managers can overcome resistance and gain buy-in from employees and stakeholders.

In conclusion, addressing concerns and overcoming resistance is crucial for the successful implementation of VR in corporate training. By educating and informing employees, addressing safety concerns, providing training and support, addressing privacy and data security concerns, involving employees in the process, and effectively communicating the benefits, HR managers can ensure a smooth transition to VR training and maximize its potential in transforming corporate training.

13.3 Overcoming Resistance to VR Adoption

Virtual Reality (VR) has the potential to revolutionize corporate training by providing immersive and engaging learning experiences. However, despite its numerous benefits, there may be resistance to adopting VR in some organizations. This resistance can stem from various concerns and challenges that need to be addressed in order to successfully implement VR training programs. In this section, we will explore some common sources of resistance and strategies to overcome them.

13.3.1 Lack of Awareness and Understanding

One of the primary reasons for resistance to VR adoption is a lack of awareness and understanding of the technology. Many decision-makers may not be familiar with the capabilities and benefits of VR in corporate training. To overcome this resistance, it is crucial to educate key stakeholders about the potential of VR and its impact on employee engagement and performance.

One effective strategy is to organize workshops or presentations to showcase the capabilities of VR in a corporate training context. By providing hands-on experiences and demonstrating the effectiveness of VR training, decision-makers can gain a better understanding of its value. Additionally, sharing case studies and success stories from companies that have already implemented VR training programs can help alleviate concerns and build confidence in the technology.

13.3.2 Cost and Return on Investment (ROI) Concerns

Another common source of resistance to VR adoption is the perceived high cost of implementing VR training programs. Decision-makers may be hesitant to invest in VR technology due to concerns about the return on investment. To overcome this resistance, it is important to demonstrate the long-term benefits and cost savings associated with VR training.

One approach is to conduct a cost-benefit analysis that compares the expenses of traditional training methods with the potential savings and improved outcomes of VR training. Highlighting the reduced need for physical training facilities, travel expenses, and instructor fees can help illustrate the cost-effectiveness of VR. Additionally, showcasing the potential for increased employee engagement, knowledge retention, and performance improvement can further justify the investment in VR training.

13.3.3 Technical Challenges and Infrastructure Requirements

Resistance to VR adoption can also arise from concerns about technical challenges and infrastructure requirements. Decision-makers may worry about the complexity of implementing and maintaining VR systems, as well as the need for specialized hardware and software. To overcome these concerns, it is important to provide comprehensive support and guidance throughout the implementation process.

Working closely with IT departments and VR technology providers can help address technical challenges and ensure a smooth integration of VR systems into existing infrastructure. Providing training and resources for IT staff and end-users can help alleviate concerns about the complexity of VR technology. Additionally, offering ongoing technical support and maintenance services can help build confidence in the reliability and sustainability of VR training programs.

13.3.4 Resistance to Change and Fear of the Unknown

Resistance to VR adoption can also stem from a general resistance to change and fear of the unknown. Some employees and stakeholders may be hesitant to embrace new technologies and may prefer traditional training methods. To overcome this resistance, it is important to address the underlying concerns and fears associated with change.

Open and transparent communication is key to overcoming resistance to change. Providing clear explanations of the benefits and objectives of VR training, as well as addressing any misconceptions or fears, can help alleviate resistance. Involving employees in the decision-making process and seeking their input and feedback can also help foster a sense of ownership and engagement.

13.3.5 Training and Support for End-Users

Resistance to VR adoption can also arise from concerns about the learning curve and usability of VR systems. Employees may worry about their ability to adapt to the new technology and may feel overwhelmed by the prospect of using VR for training purposes. To overcome this resistance, it is important to provide comprehensive training and support for end-users.

Offering training sessions and workshops that focus on the basics of VR technology and its use in training can help employees feel more comfortable and confident. Providing user-friendly interfaces and intuitive controls can also help simplify the learning process. Additionally, offering ongoing support and troubleshooting resources can help address any issues or challenges that arise during the implementation and use of VR training programs.

By addressing these common sources of resistance and implementing effective strategies, organizations can overcome barriers to VR adoption and unlock the full potential of immersive learning in corporate training.

13.4 Communicating the Value of VR Training

Virtual Reality (VR) has the potential to revolutionize corporate training by providing immersive and engaging learning experiences. However, introducing VR into an organization's training program may face resistance and skepticism from stakeholders. To successfully implement VR training, it is crucial to effectively communicate the value and benefits it brings. In this section, we will explore strategies for effectively communicating the value of VR training to key stakeholders.

13.4.1 Understanding Stakeholder Perspectives

Before communicating the value of VR training, it is important to understand the perspectives and concerns of key stakeholders. Different stakeholders may have different priorities and expectations, so tailoring the communication approach to each group is essential. Here are some common stakeholders and their potential concerns:

13.4.1.1 Senior Management

Senior management is primarily concerned with the return on investment (ROI) and the impact on the organization's bottom line. They may question the cost-effectiveness of implementing VR training and the potential benefits it brings to the organization.

13.4.1.2 HR Managers

HR managers are responsible for designing and implementing training programs. They may be concerned about the feasibility of integrating VR into existing training methods, the impact on employee engagement and performance, and the potential challenges in managing the VR training program.

13.4.1.3 Employees

Employees are the end-users of VR training. They may have concerns about the learning curve associated with using VR technology, the relevance of VR training to their job roles, and the impact on their daily work routines.

13.4.2 Tailoring the Message

To effectively communicate the value of VR training, it is important to tailor the message to address the specific concerns and priorities of each stakeholder group. Here are some strategies for tailoring the message:

13.4.2.1 Senior Management

When communicating with senior management, focus on the potential ROI and the long-term benefits of VR training. Highlight how VR can improve employee performance, reduce training costs, and enhance the organization's competitive advantage. Provide data and case studies from other companies that have successfully implemented VR training to support your arguments.

13.4.2.2 HR Managers

When communicating with HR managers, emphasize the practical benefits of VR training. Highlight how VR can enhance the effectiveness of training programs, improve employee engagement and retention, and provide a more immersive and realistic learning experience. Address any concerns about integrating VR into existing training methods by showcasing successful case studies and providing guidance on implementation strategies.

13.4.2.3 Employees

When communicating with employees, focus on the benefits of VR training from their perspective. Highlight how VR can provide a more engaging and interactive learning experience, allowing them to practice real-life scenarios in a safe and controlled environment. Address any concerns about the learning curve by emphasizing the user-friendly nature of VR technology and providing training and support resources.

13.4.3 Demonstrating the Value

In addition to tailoring the message, it is important to demonstrate the value of VR training through practical examples and hands-on experiences. Here are some strategies for demonstrating the value of VR training:

13.4.3.1 Pilot Programs

Implementing pilot programs can be an effective way to demonstrate the value of VR training. Select a small group of employees or a specific department to participate in a VR training program and collect feedback and data on the impact of VR training on their performance and engagement. Use this data to showcase the benefits of VR training to other stakeholders.

13.4.3.2 Virtual Tours and Demonstrations

Organize virtual tours and demonstrations to allow stakeholders to experience VR training firsthand. Create immersive VR experiences that showcase the potential applications of VR training in different job roles and industries. This can help stakeholders understand the value and benefits of VR training in a more tangible way.

13.4.3.3 Case Studies and Success Stories

Share case studies and success stories from other companies that have successfully implemented VR training. Highlight the positive outcomes, such as improved employee performance, increased engagement, and cost savings. Use these examples to illustrate the potential benefits of VR training and build credibility.

13.4.4 Continuous Communication and Education

Effective communication is an ongoing process. It is important to continuously communicate and educate stakeholders about the value of VR training. Provide regular updates on the progress of VR training programs, share success stories and testimonials from employees, and address any concerns or questions that arise. This will help build trust and support for VR training initiatives.

By tailoring the message, demonstrating the value, and maintaining continuous communication and education, HR managers can effectively communicate the value of VR training to key stakeholders. This will help overcome resistance and skepticism and pave the way for successful implementation of VR training programs in the organization.

Future Trends in VR Corporate Training

14.1 Emerging Technologies and Innovations

Virtual reality (VR) has already made a significant impact on corporate training, revolutionizing the way employees learn and develop new skills. However, the field of VR is constantly evolving, and new technologies and innovations are emerging that promise to further enhance the effectiveness and efficiency of VR training programs. In this section, we will explore some of these emerging technologies and innovations and discuss their potential applications in the future of VR corporate training.

14.1.1 Artificial Intelligence and Machine Learning

Artificial intelligence (AI) and machine learning (ML) are two rapidly advancing technologies that have the potential to greatly enhance the capabilities of VR training programs. By incorporating AI and ML algorithms into VR simulations, training experiences can become more personalized and adaptive to individual learners. AI can analyze user behavior and performance data in real-time, providing instant feedback and customized learning paths. ML algorithms can also be used to create intelligent virtual characters that can interact with trainees, providing realistic scenarios and dynamic responses.

One of the key benefits of AI and ML in VR training is the ability to track and analyze trainee performance data. By collecting data on trainee behavior, such as gaze patterns, movement, and decision-making, AI algorithms can identify areas of improvement and provide targeted feedback. This data-driven approach allows for continuous assessment and personalized learning experiences, ensuring that trainees receive the most relevant and effective training.

14.1.2 Augmented Reality Integration

While VR provides a fully immersive experience, augmented reality (AR) overlays digital information onto the real world, creating a blended environment. The integration of AR with VR training programs can offer unique opportunities for hands-on learning and real-time feedback. For example, trainees can use AR-enabled devices to interact with virtual objects in their physical environment, enhancing the realism and practicality of the training experience.

AR integration can also enable collaborative training scenarios, where multiple trainees can interact with each other and virtual objects in a shared space. This fosters teamwork and communication skills, which are essential in many corporate settings. Additionally, AR can provide contextual information and guidance during training, helping trainees navigate complex tasks and procedures more effectively.

14.1.3 Haptic Feedback and Sensory Stimulation

Haptic feedback technology allows users to feel and touch virtual objects, enhancing the sense of presence and realism in VR simulations. By incorporating haptic feedback devices, such as gloves or suits, into VR training programs, trainees can experience tactile sensations that mimic real-world interactions. This technology is particularly valuable in training scenarios that require precise motor skills or physical manipulation of objects.

In addition to haptic feedback, advancements in sensory stimulation technologies are also contributing to the immersive nature of VR training. For example, olfactory devices can release scents that correspond to specific virtual environments, enhancing the trainee's sensory experience. Similarly, auditory systems can provide realistic soundscapes, further immersing trainees in the virtual environment.

14.1.4 Eye-Tracking and Biometric Sensors

Eye-tracking technology allows for the measurement and analysis of a trainee's gaze patterns and attentional focus during VR training. By tracking eye movements, trainers can gain insights into trainee engagement, cognitive load, and decision-making processes. This information can be used to optimize training content and improve the effectiveness of VR simulations.

Biometric sensors, such as heart rate monitors and electrodermal activity sensors, can provide additional data on trainee physiological responses. By monitoring trainee stress levels and emotional states, trainers can tailor the training experience to individual needs and ensure optimal learning outcomes. These technologies can also be used to create adaptive training scenarios that dynamically adjust based on trainee's physiological responses.

14.1.5 Cloud-Based VR Training Platforms

Cloud-based VR training platforms offer several advantages over traditional on-premises solutions. By leveraging the power of cloud computing, these platforms can deliver high-quality VR experiences to trainees without the need for expensive hardware or software installations. This makes VR training more accessible and scalable for organizations of all sizes.

Cloud-based platforms also enable real-time collaboration and remote training sessions, allowing geographically dispersed teams to participate in the same VR training program. This is particularly beneficial for global organizations that need to train employees located in different regions. Furthermore, cloud-based platforms can facilitate the collection and analysis of training data, providing valuable insights into trainee performance and program effectiveness.

Conclusion

As VR technology continues to evolve, so does its potential for transforming corporate training. Emerging technologies such as artificial intelligence, augmented reality integration, haptic feedback, eye-tracking, and cloud-based platforms are revolutionizing the way employees learn and develop new skills. By embracing these innovations, organizations can create more immersive, personalized, and effective VR training programs. HR and training professionals should stay informed about these emerging technologies and be prepared to adapt their training strategies to leverage their full potential. The future of VR corporate training holds exciting possibilities, and organizations that embrace these innovations will be at the forefront of the immersive learning revolution.

14.2 Potential Applications of VR in the Future

Virtual Reality (VR) has already made a significant impact on corporate training, revolutionizing the way employees learn and develop new skills. As technology continues to advance, the potential applications of VR in the future are vast and exciting. In this section, we will explore some of the potential areas where VR can further enhance corporate training.

14.2.1 Virtual Reality for Soft Skills Training

While VR has been predominantly used for technical and job-specific training, its potential for soft skills development is immense. Soft skills, such as communication, leadership, and teamwork, are crucial for success in the workplace. VR can provide immersive environments where employees can practice and refine these skills in realistic scenarios.

For example, VR simulations can recreate challenging customer service interactions, allowing employees to practice their communication and problem-solving skills in a safe and controlled environment. VR can also simulate team-building exercises, enabling employees to collaborate and develop effective teamwork skills.

14.2.2 Virtual Reality for Diversity and Inclusion Training

Diversity and inclusion are essential aspects of modern workplaces. VR can play a significant role in promoting understanding and empathy among employees by providing immersive experiences that simulate different perspectives and experiences.

For instance, VR can create scenarios where employees can step into the shoes of individuals from diverse backgrounds and experience the challenges they face. This can help foster empathy, reduce biases, and promote a more inclusive work environment.

14.2.3 Virtual Reality for Leadership Development

Leadership development is a critical area where VR can have a profound impact. VR simulations can provide aspiring leaders with opportunities to practice decision-making, conflict resolution, and strategic thinking in realistic scenarios.

By immersing leaders in challenging situations, VR can help them develop their leadership skills and gain valuable experience without the risk of real-world consequences. VR can also facilitate leadership training programs by allowing participants to interact with virtual mentors and receive personalized feedback and guidance.

14.2.4 Virtual Reality for Onboarding and Orientation

Onboarding new employees can be a time-consuming and costly process. VR can streamline this process by providing immersive onboarding experiences that familiarize new hires with the company culture, policies, and procedures.

Through VR, new employees can explore virtual office spaces, interact with virtual colleagues, and participate in simulated work tasks. This can help them feel more comfortable and confident in their new roles, leading to faster integration and productivity.

14.2.5 Virtual Reality for Remote and Distributed Workforces

With the rise of remote and distributed workforces, VR can bridge the gap between physical and virtual collaboration. VR can create virtual meeting spaces where remote employees can come together, interact, and collaborate as if they were in the same room.

By providing a sense of presence and immersion, VR can enhance communication and teamwork among remote teams. It can also facilitate virtual training sessions, workshops, and conferences, eliminating the need for travel and reducing costs.

14.2.6 Virtual Reality for Safety Training

Safety training is a critical aspect of many industries, such as manufacturing, construction, and healthcare. VR can provide realistic and immersive simulations of hazardous situations, allowing employees to practice safety protocols and emergency procedures in a controlled environment.

By experiencing potential risks and hazards in VR, employees can develop the necessary skills and knowledge to respond effectively in real-life situations. VR can also track and analyze performance, providing valuable data for evaluating and improving safety training programs.

14.2.7 Virtual Reality for Continuous Learning and Professional Development

In the future, VR can play a significant role in enabling continuous learning and professional development. VR simulations can provide employees with ongoing opportunities to practice and refine their skills, ensuring they stay up to date with industry trends and best practices.

By incorporating AI and machine learning, VR can personalize learning experiences, adapting to individual needs and preferences. VR can also facilitate virtual mentorship programs, connecting employees with experienced professionals who can provide guidance and support.

The potential applications of VR in corporate training are vast and continually evolving. As technology advances and becomes more accessible, organizations can leverage VR to create immersive and engaging learning experiences that drive employee performance and development. By embracing these future trends, HR and training professionals can stay ahead of the curve and unlock the full potential of VR in corporate training.

14.3 Implications for HR and Training Professionals

As virtual reality (VR) continues to revolutionize corporate training, HR and training professionals are faced with new opportunities and challenges. The implications of VR in the field of HR and training are vast, and understanding these implications is crucial for professionals looking to leverage this technology effectively. In this section, we will explore the key implications of VR for HR and training professionals and discuss how they can adapt to this transformative technology.

14.3.1 Redefining Training Methods

One of the most significant implications of VR for HR and training professionals is the redefinition of traditional training methods. VR offers a highly immersive and interactive learning experience that goes beyond traditional classroom-based or e-learning approaches. With VR, employees can engage in realistic simulations, allowing them to practice and apply their skills in a safe and controlled environment. This shift in training methods requires HR and training professionals to rethink their approach to curriculum design, content development, and delivery.

14.3.2 Enhancing Employee Engagement

Employee engagement is a critical factor in the success of any training program. VR has the potential to significantly enhance employee engagement by providing a more immersive and interactive learning experience. By placing employees in realistic scenarios and allowing them to actively participate in the learning process, VR training can capture and maintain their attention more effectively. HR and training professionals can leverage this increased engagement to improve knowledge retention, skill acquisition, and overall training outcomes.

14.3.3 Personalized and Adaptive Learning

VR technology enables personalized and adaptive learning experiences, catering to the individual needs and learning styles of employees. Through VR, HR and training professionals can create customized training programs that adapt to each employee's skill level, learning pace, and preferences. This personalized approach not only enhances the effectiveness of training but also empowers employees to take ownership of their learning journey. HR and training professionals need to embrace this shift towards personalized and adaptive learning and explore ways to leverage VR technology to its full potential.

14.3.4 Data-Driven Training Insights

Another significant implication of VR for HR and training professionals is the availability of data-driven training insights. VR training platforms can collect a wealth of data, including employee performance metrics, engagement levels, and learning progress. By analyzing this data, HR and training professionals can gain valuable insights into the effectiveness of their training programs, identify areas for improvement, and make data-driven decisions to optimize training outcomes. This data-driven approach to training can lead to more targeted and impactful learning experiences for employees.

14.3.5 Collaboration and Remote Training

VR technology also opens up new possibilities for collaboration and remote training. With VR, HR and training professionals can create virtual environments where employees from different locations can come together and collaborate on training activities. This is particularly beneficial for organizations with geographically dispersed teams or remote workers. HR and training professionals can leverage VR to facilitate virtual meetings, team-building exercises, and interactive training sessions, fostering collaboration and teamwork regardless of physical distance.

14.3.6 Continuous Learning and Skill Development

In today's rapidly evolving business landscape, continuous learning and skill development are essential for employees to stay competitive. VR offers a powerful tool for continuous learning, allowing HR and training professionals to provide ongoing training and skill development opportunities. With VR, employees can access training modules and simulations at any time, enabling them to continuously enhance their skills and knowledge. HR and training professionals need to embrace this shift towards continuous learning and leverage VR to create a culture of lifelong learning within their organizations.

14.3.7 Upskilling and Reskilling

The rapid advancement of technology often requires employees to upskill or reskill to meet the changing demands of their roles. VR can play a crucial role in upskilling and reskilling initiatives by providing employees with hands-on training experiences in new technologies or processes. HR and training professionals can leverage VR to create immersive training programs that enable employees to acquire new skills or adapt existing ones. By embracing VR for upskilling and reskilling, HR and training professionals can ensure that their workforce remains agile and adaptable in the face of technological advancements.

14.3.8 Change Management and Adoption

Introducing VR into corporate training requires effective change management and adoption strategies. HR and training professionals need to proactively address any resistance or concerns from employees and stakeholders. Clear communication about the benefits and value of VR training is crucial to gaining buy-in and support. Additionally, providing adequate training and support to employees during the transition to VR-based training is essential for successful adoption. HR and training professionals should develop comprehensive change management plans and provide ongoing support to ensure a smooth transition to VR training.

In conclusion, the implications of VR for HR and training professionals are vast and transformative. By redefining training methods, enhancing employee engagement, enabling personalized and adaptive learning, leveraging data-driven insights, facilitating collaboration and remote training, promoting continuous learning and skill development, supporting upskilling and reskilling initiatives, and effectively managing change and adoption, HR and training professionals can harness the full potential of VR to transform corporate training and drive organizational success.

14.4 Preparing for the Future of VR Training

As virtual reality (VR) continues to evolve and advance, it is crucial for HR and training professionals to stay ahead of the curve and prepare for the future of VR training. The rapid pace of technological advancements and the increasing demand for immersive learning experiences necessitate a proactive approach in order to fully leverage the potential of VR in corporate training. In this section, we will explore some key considerations and strategies to help you prepare for the future of VR training.

14.4.1 Embracing Continuous Learning and Adaptability

One of the fundamental aspects of preparing for the future of VR training is embracing a culture of continuous learning and adaptability. As new technologies and innovations emerge, it is essential for HR and training professionals to stay informed and up to date with the latest trends and developments in the field of VR. This can be achieved through attending industry conferences, participating in webinars, and engaging with VR communities and forums. By fostering a mindset of continuous learning, you can ensure that your organization remains at the forefront of VR training.

14.4.2 Investing in Research and Development

To effectively prepare for the future of VR training, it is important to allocate resources for research and development. By investing in R&D, you can explore new possibilities and experiment with cutting-edge technologies that have the potential to enhance the effectiveness of VR training programs. This may involve collaborating with VR developers, universities, or research institutions to explore innovative applications of VR in corporate training. By actively engaging in R&D, you can gain valuable insights and identify new opportunities for leveraging VR in your organization's training initiatives.

14.4.3 Anticipating Technological Advancements

The field of VR is constantly evolving, with new technologies and advancements being introduced regularly. To prepare for the future of VR training, it is crucial to anticipate these technological advancements and understand their potential impact on corporate training. This requires staying informed about emerging VR hardware, software, and development tools. By keeping a pulse on the latest advancements, you can make informed decisions about when and how to integrate new technologies into your VR training programs.

14.4.4 Adapting Training Strategies to VR

As VR technology continues to advance, it is important to adapt training strategies to fully leverage its potential. Traditional training methods may not be suitable for VR, and therefore, it is necessary to rethink and redesign training programs to align with the immersive nature of VR. This may involve creating interactive and engaging VR scenarios, incorporating gamification elements, and leveraging the full range of sensory experiences that VR can offer. By adapting training strategies to VR, you can maximize the impact and effectiveness of your VR training programs.

14.4.5 Upskilling HR and Training Professionals

Preparing for the future of VR training also involves upskilling HR and training professionals to effectively utilize VR technology. This may require providing training and development opportunities for HR and training professionals to enhance their understanding of VR and its applications in corporate training. By equipping your team with the necessary skills and knowledge, you can ensure that they are well-prepared to design, implement, and manage VR training programs in the future.

14.4.6 Collaborating with VR Experts and Developers

To stay ahead in the field of VR training, it is beneficial to collaborate with VR experts and developers. By partnering with experienced VR professionals, you can gain valuable insights, access specialized knowledge, and leverage their expertise in designing and implementing VR training programs. Collaborating with VR experts and developers can also help you navigate the rapidly evolving VR landscape and ensure that your organization remains at the forefront of VR training innovation.

14.4.7 Monitoring Industry Trends and Best Practices

To effectively prepare for the future of VR training, it is important to monitor industry trends and best practices. This involves staying informed about the latest advancements, case studies, and success stories in the field of VR training. By keeping a close eye on industry trends and best practices, you can gain inspiration, learn from the experiences of other organizations, and identify new opportunities for enhancing your own VR training programs.

14.4.8 Evaluating and Measuring the Impact of VR Training

As VR training becomes more prevalent, it is crucial to evaluate and measure its impact on employee performance and engagement. By implementing robust evaluation and measurement strategies, you can gather data and insights to assess the effectiveness of your VR training programs. This may involve conducting pre and post-training assessments, gathering feedback from trainees, and analyzing performance metrics. By continuously evaluating and measuring the impact of VR training, you can make data-driven decisions and continuously improve your VR training initiatives.

In conclusion, preparing for the future of VR training requires a proactive and forward-thinking approach. By embracing continuous learning, investing in research and development, anticipating technological advancements, adapting training strategies, upskilling HR and training professionals, collaborating with VR experts, monitoring industry trends, and evaluating the impact of VR training, you can position your organization for success in the ever-evolving landscape of VR corporate training.

Conclusion

15.1 Summary of Key Points

In this book, we have explored the transformative power of virtual reality (VR) in corporate training. We have discussed the various aspects of VR technology, its benefits, challenges, and considerations. We have also delved into the impact of VR on employee engagement, the implementation strategies, and the building of VR training programs. Additionally, we have examined several case studies of companies that have successfully integrated VR into their training programs. In this final section, we will summarize the key points discussed throughout the book and provide some final thoughts and recommendations.

15.1.1 The Power of Virtual Reality in Corporate Training

Virtual reality has the potential to revolutionize corporate training by providing immersive and interactive learning experiences. It allows employees to engage with realistic scenarios, practice skills in a safe environment, and receive immediate feedback. VR can enhance the learning experience, increase motivation and retention, improve skills acquisition and application, and foster collaboration and teamwork.

15.1.2 Implementing VR in HR Strategies

To successfully implement VR in HR strategies, organizations need to assess their training needs and objectives. They should design VR training programs that align with their goals and integrate VR into existing training methods. Measuring the effectiveness of VR training is crucial to ensure its impact on employee performance and engagement.

15.1.3 Building Your VR Training Program

Building a VR training program involves identifying VR training opportunities, selecting appropriate content, creating realistic and engaging scenarios, and implementing the necessary infrastructure. Organizations should consider the specific needs of their employees and tailor the VR training program accordingly.

15.1.4 Case Studies: Success Stories

Throughout the book, we have examined several case studies of companies that have successfully implemented VR in their training programs. Johnson & Johnson, Chevron, Bank of America, Verizon, Hilton, DHL, and Presbyterian New York Hospital have all experienced positive outcomes from their VR training initiatives. These case studies provide valuable insights into the success factors and lessons learned from each organization's journey.

15.1.5 Addressing Concerns and Overcoming Resistance

While VR has immense potential, there are common concerns and resistance to its adoption in corporate training. Organizations need to address these concerns by providing clear communication, addressing privacy and safety issues, and demonstrating the value of VR training. Strategies for overcoming resistance include involving key stakeholders, providing training and support, and showcasing success stories.

15.1.6 Future Trends in VR Corporate Training

As technology continues to evolve, so does the potential for VR in corporate training. Emerging technologies and innovations, such as augmented reality and artificial intelligence, are likely to shape the future of VR training. HR and training professionals need to stay informed about these trends and prepare for the future by investing in the necessary infrastructure and resources.

15.1.7 Final Thoughts and Recommendations

In conclusion, virtual reality has the power to transform corporate training by providing immersive and engaging learning experiences. By implementing VR in HR strategies, organizations can enhance employee engagement, improve performance, and drive business results. Building a successful VR training program requires careful planning, consideration of specific needs, and effective measurement of outcomes. Addressing concerns and overcoming resistance is crucial for successful adoption. Finally, staying informed about future trends and preparing for technological advancements will ensure organizations stay ahead in the ever-evolving world of VR corporate training. As you embark on your journey to introduce virtual reality into your corporate training programs, we hope this book has provided you with the knowledge and guidance needed to navigate the challenges and unlock the full potential of immersive learning. Good luck on your VR revolution!

15.2 Final Thoughts and Recommendations

As we conclude this book, it is evident that virtual reality (VR) has the potential to revolutionize corporate training. Throughout the chapters, we have explored the foundations of VR, its impact on employee engagement, strategies for implementing VR in HR, and case studies of companies that have successfully integrated VR into their training programs. In this final section, we will provide some final thoughts and recommendations to guide you in your journey towards leveraging the power of VR in corporate training.

15.2.1 Embracing the Paradigm Shift

Virtual reality represents a paradigm shift in the way we approach corporate training. It offers a unique opportunity to create immersive and interactive learning experiences that engage employees on a whole new level. As you embark on this journey, it is crucial to embrace this shift and recognize the potential that VR holds for transforming your training programs.

15.2.2 Start with a Clear Vision and Strategy

Before diving into VR implementation, it is essential to have a clear vision and strategy in place. Define your training objectives, identify the areas where VR can make the most significant impact, and align your VR training program with your overall HR strategy. By starting with a well-defined plan, you can ensure that your VR training initiatives are purposeful and aligned with your organizational goals.

15.2.3 Collaborate with Subject Matter Experts

To create effective VR training content, it is crucial to collaborate with subject matter experts (SMEs) from within your organization. SMEs possess the knowledge and expertise required to design realistic and relevant training scenarios. By involving them in the content creation process, you can ensure that your VR training program accurately reflects the challenges and situations that employees encounter in their roles.

15.2.4 Prioritize User Experience

User experience should be at the forefront of your VR training program. Design intuitive and user-friendly interfaces that allow employees to navigate the virtual environment seamlessly. Consider the comfort and safety of your users by providing appropriate training equipment and ensuring that the VR experience does not cause discomfort or motion sickness. By prioritizing user experience, you can enhance engagement and maximize the effectiveness of your VR training.

15.2.5 Continuously Evaluate and Improve

As with any training program, it is essential to continuously evaluate the effectiveness of your VR training initiatives. Collect feedback from employees, track performance metrics, and analyze the impact of VR on employee engagement and skill acquisition. Use this data to identify areas for improvement and make necessary adjustments to your VR training program. By adopting a continuous improvement mindset, you can ensure that your VR training remains relevant and impactful.

15.2.6 Foster a Culture of Learning and Innovation

Introducing VR into your corporate training program is not just about implementing a new technology; it is about fostering a culture of learning and innovation within your organization. Encourage employees to embrace new technologies and explore the possibilities that VR offers for their professional development. By creating a supportive environment that values continuous learning and innovation, you can drive employee engagement and empower your workforce to reach their full potential.

15.2.7 Stay Ahead of the Curve

The field of VR is rapidly evolving, and new technologies and innovations are emerging at an unprecedented pace. To stay ahead of the curve, it is crucial to stay informed about the latest trends and developments in VR. Attend industry conferences, join professional networks, and engage with VR experts to stay updated on the latest advancements. By staying ahead of the curve, you can ensure that your VR training program remains cutting-edge and continues to deliver value to your organization.

15.2.8 Seek Inspiration from Case Studies

Throughout this book, we have explored case studies of companies that have successfully implemented VR in their training programs. These case studies provide valuable insights and lessons learned that can inspire and guide your own VR initiatives. Take the time to study these case studies, understand the success factors, and adapt the strategies that align with your organization's unique needs and challenges.

15.2.9 Collaboration and Knowledge Sharing

Lastly, we encourage you to collaborate and share your experiences with other HR professionals and organizations that are exploring VR in corporate training. By sharing knowledge and best practices, we can collectively advance the field of VR training and drive innovation in corporate learning. Join industry forums, participate in webinars, and engage in discussions to contribute to the collective knowledge and benefit from the experiences of others.

In conclusion, the potential of virtual reality in corporate training is immense. By leveraging the power of VR, organizations can create immersive and engaging learning experiences that enhance employee engagement, improve skills acquisition, and foster collaboration. As you embark on your VR journey, remember to start with a clear vision, prioritize user experience, continuously evaluate and improve, and foster a culture of learning and innovation. By following these recommendations and staying ahead of the curve, you can unlock the full potential of VR in transforming your corporate training programs.

Summary